Practical Reading
Some new remedial techniques

Practical Reading
Some new remedial techniques

James Webster
Director, the Reading Clinic, Jersey
Sometime Lecturer in Education,
Newton Park College, Bath
Sometime Senior Lecturer in Education,
Redland College, Bristol

Evans Brothers Limited, London

Published by
Evans Brothers Limited,
Montague House, Russell Square, London, W.C.1

Set in 11 on 12 pt. Imprint and printed in Gt. Britain
by The Camelot Press Ltd., London and Southampton
57/6678   PR 2528

Acknowledgements

The author acknowledges with thanks the permission of the British Broadcasting Corporation to include in the first two chapters parts of four scripts originally broadcast in *Parents and Children* (Network Three) and *Woman's Hour* (Light Programme).

Acknowledgement is also made to *The Teacher* for permission to reprint Dramatic Reading (Chapter 6) and details of the three techniques described in Chapter 10.

The author is further indebted to *Teacher's World* for permission to include in other parts of this book excerpts that first appeared in article form.

The cartoon of *Freddy* is reproduced by kind permission of Bob Bennett and the Bristol *Evening Post* and the cartoon of Fred Basset is reproduced by kind permission of the *Daily Mail*.

Contents

Introduction

There are, we may feel, far too many volumes already on this vexed topic of the teaching of reading, which is perhaps an unfortunate way of introducing yet another book on the same subject.

The overwhelming majority of such books, however, make their primary concern the *theory* of teaching reading, or, worse still, the academic justification of sundry reading schemes. But this little book has rather a different outlook. It has been written to answer a fundamental question that inevitably arises when teachers get together to discuss the teaching of reading: 'What do you DO about children who cannot read?'

This, after all, is what really matters. The vast background of research literature is fascinating to explore, and a sound grasp of theoretical principles is worth a great deal in remedial work. An understanding of children, their development and problems, is even more valuable. But, in the hurly-burly of the crowded classroom, all too often an ounce of practical know-how outweighs a ton of theory. 'Whys' and 'wherefores' are all very well, but at five to nine on a Monday morning, WHAT TO DO? is the question that has to be answered.

PRACTICAL READING is basically a collection of classroom techniques that have proved effective in tackling this

ever-present stumbling block of difficulty with reading. Some
are patently simple, others a little less so. Some are mainly
phonic in outlook, others are linked to Look-and-Say. We
hold no brief for any one particular approach to the exclu-
sion of all others, an attitude which has frequently proved
to be the hall-mark of the theorist. Anything and everything
that can usefully be employed to the end of helping children
is acceptable to us. In fact, most experienced teachers would
reject with a pardonably cynical smile the idea that one
'magic' method could provide a complete answer to reading
difficulty.

This may seem inconsistent with the amount of space
which later we devote to the consideration of V-V, or Visual-
Verbal Method, but there we will be dealing with something
completely new in concept and background, and with very
wide possibilities of application.

V-V arose from the needs of Word-blind children, whose
particular weaknesses rendered the conventional visual im-
pact of Look-and-Say nearly useless. It is a method in its
own right, as distinct from a technique or scheme in the
narrower sense of these terms. Nevertheless, it still remains *a*
method.

In the practical field, V-V, in common with all the other
suggestions we shall put forward, will find both support and
opposition, approval and rejection, which is as it should be.
We would not like to think that every remedial suggestion
put forward will meet with universal approval, since the
success or lack of success with any given technique depends
to a large extent on the particular difficulties of the child
concerned—*and the attitude and skill of the teacher.*

In general, what we believe is going to work *will* work;
what we feel at the bottom of our hearts to be a sheer waste
of time will in all probability turn out to be just that. But
let us hope that those whose classes contain a single child
who cannot read, as well as those whose classes lack a single

child who can, will find in the pages that follow at least the beginnings of a practical answer to this urgent question of 'What do you actually do?'

And if there are little bits of theory popping out here and there, well, we are perfectly free to read what catches our interest, and to turn the page that fails to appeal.

As are the children we teach.

Some Thoughts Before We Begin

"A child capable of learning to understand speech by associating sound symbols with meaning therefore demonstrates his capacity to learn to read which merely offers him seen symbols and patterns instead of heard ones."
(J. Hemming. *Ready Reading for Backward Readers*. Longmans. 1951.)

"Recent surveys have shown a decrease in the frequency of reading backwardness, but at 11 years about 1 per cent are still almost totally illiterate and about 20 per cent considerably retarded. About 19 per cent of entrants to Junior Schools are virtually non-readers."
(Prof. M. D. Vernon in a lecture to the International Reading Association, London, 1963.)

"And how do the educators explain all the thousands and thousands of remedial cases? This is what really got me mad. To them, failure in reading is *never* caused by poor teaching. Lord, no. Perish the thought! Reading failure is due to poor eyesight, or a nervous stomach, or poor posture, or heredity, or a broken home, or undernourishment, or a wicked stepmother, or an Oedipus complex, or sibling rivalry, or God knows what. The teacher or the school are never at fault!"
(Flesch. *Why Johnny can't Read*. Harper. 1955.)

"The Infants' Schools' reputation for the highest standards of teaching skill is well known and well deserved. The fault therefore seems likely to lie outside their control, and to be one that is common to the various methods currently used for the teaching of reading."
(J. Downing. *To bee or not to be*. Cassell. 1962.)

"It is often impossible to adopt modern methods of teaching because teachers are not adequately trained."
(Gray. *The teaching of Reading and Writing*. Unesco. 1956.)

"*Backwards* Readers? Not that I know of. They all read *forwards* here. I think . . ." (School Secretary on the telephone.)

Chapter 1

First Things First

"The whole point about being a human being is communication."—
Sir Edward Boyle

Anyone glancing over the next page or two will see with
half an eye that, despite all the promises made in the introduction, this book has started off in the good old theoretical
fashion.

Yet is there any way round this little bit of initial theory?
Suppose, for example, that we have a motor car that has a
very poor performance, or that won't start at all. Suppose
that we decide to put things right ourselves. If we know little
or nothing about car engines, we would be unwise—to say
the least—to touch anything at all until we had made ourselves familiar with the way in which the engine functions
normally. In fact, we could easily make things worse.

The same applies to a doctor. Before he is in a position
to diagnose and treat diseases and abnormalities of the body,
he must know how the various organs, systems and so on
function and appear in the ordinary run of events. Similarly,
if we are to help children with troubles and difficulties in
reading, we must have a clear understanding of what this
miracle of communication called Reading consists of, and
how it is normally acquired. We shall also need to think about

the reasons and conditions which lead to the Reading Failure.

Few people realise just what a miracle this business of extracting meaning from patterns of squiggles on a sheet of paper really is. An idea comes into a man's head. It is something vague, tenuous and fleeting: a crystallisation, distillation, and a regrouping of past experience in the form of thought.

Thoughts can go as quickly as they come. They can be forgotten; lost for ever in that apparently bottomless pit of the subconscious. Or we can shake them about until they settle down into the accepted mounds of groups of sounds called sentences. Yet these sentences, once uttered, vanish into thin air. They, too, may escape recall.

But if these words are written down, they are there for good. By using various combinations of twenty-six awkward little squiggles called letters (in this country and until we adopt a more logical alphabet) we can trap thought, news, views, feeling, knowledge, pleasure and emotion in a paper cage. Through the act of reading, one person may make contact with the mind and world of another. This is a connection of thought and experience that takes no account of place, or time, or distance or death. It is talking with Plato and seeing "No Parking" warnings. It is keeping in touch with Susan in Australia and sharing Scott's last thoughts and feelings in that tiny little tent in the middle of nowhere. It is the very root of Man's progress and the nervous system of his civilisation. It is indeed a miracle.

Perhaps people who cannot read are better qualified to judge the real value of the printed word. It is they who realise fully what it is like to be cut off from the world of everyday communication. To be locked out of the humour, adventure, fantasy and knowledge that makes up the realm of books. To be kept in the dark as to what is going on but to see only too clearly that they are social outcasts—'inferior' beings; people who 'cannot even read'.

And since all this applies equally—if not more so—to children, can we wonder if the non-readers, the backward readers and the retarded readers find their struggles complicated and hampered by their feelings? Feelings, we should note in passing, that are denied the socially acceptable safety valve provided by comics, thrillers and other reading material through which children can get rid of surplus emotional steam.

Heaven forbid that this should read like a chapter from a text book on the psychology of reading, but already we cannot avoid seeing that the basic, fundamental problem in remedial reading work is a human one. The first thing that has to be done is to make contact with the child *as a person*, as distinct from a non-reader. To get to know his interests, ambitions and hobbies, and to understand his nagging doubts, fears and worries.

Psychology, as far as the practising teacher confronted with children who cannot read is concerned, might well be defined as 'It ain't what you do, it's the *why* that you do it'. And in nine cases out of ten the *why* behind lack of progress in reading can be summed up in one short phrase: lack of confidence.

This in turn, it is patently obvious, means that our primary aim in any remedial work should be to boost the weak reader's confidence to the point where he no longer feels weak, inadequate, frightened and inferior (which is how he does feel, despite all the compensatory bluster, arrogance and 'silliness' that he may display).

The way to achieve this—and how easy it is just to say it—is somehow or other to make certain that as quickly as possible the weak reader tastes *success*. Not success with some other activity such as sport, although this does of course help, but with reading itself. Which may seem a bit like saying that if only the non-reader can read he is half-way to overcoming his difficulties! But this in fact is the aim of all the techniques which will be described in the following chapters.

B

To prove to the child that reading is not beyond him. That it can be fun. That it isn't as impossibly difficult as continuous failure has conditioned him to believe it to be.

Which is where we came in. We have still to examine the mechanics of the miracle.

Let us suppose that we are waiting for a friend outside Paddington station in the rush hour. There are thousands and thousands of strange faces streaming past, all composed of pretty much the same arrangement of eyes, lips, noses, ears and what have you, yet suddenly there he—or she—is. We recognise the particular face of our friend even though the facial features are arranged in much the same way as those of the throng surrounding it.

This instant recognition takes place as the result of our having seen the face of our friend a sufficient number of times to know its particular, individual pattern. Despite the conventional positioning of the framework of features there are still little differences which proclaim this face to be one we know very well. 'Jim!' we say, or 'Jill!'

Print the word *Jim* on one piece of card and *Jill* on another and a child can be told that the first one is Jim and the second Jill. And he will then be able to 'read' these two words.

What he will remember, how he will tell one word face from the other, is by thinking along these lines: 'Short, fat shape with a hook on the front—Jim! Bit longer shape with a hook on the front and two tall things sticking up at the back—Jill!' Or he may even begin by simply noticing that *Jill* is slightly longer than *Jim*.

Put a picture of a boy over the word *Jim* and a picture of a girl over *Jill* and the child will be able to see for himself what the words say, after, of course, some preliminary discussion about this boy Jim and his friend Jill—what sort of people they are, where they live, the games they play and so on. Words have to be brought to life, filled with meaning and interest for children before they are ready to be encountered in the form of print.

As the result of encountering these two words over and over again, the child will gradually become more and more familiar with their 'faces' and he will be able to pick them out even when they are surrounded by other similar words. In some ways, words have a more distinctive pattern than faces, since their 26 'features' can be arranged in an almost infinite number of patterns, each with its own unique letter sequence, length and overall shape.

Looking at the picture and saying the whole word underneath is one of the primary ways of teaching reading. 'Look-and-Say', or 'Word Whole' methods preserve meaning, and without meaning there is little point to the act of reading anyway.

The maximum amount of reading and interest is best created through the logical extension of a single word into a complete sentence. The sentence is the natural unit of meaningful thought. We speak in sentences, and so *I am Jim*, *I am Jill*, despite the addition of two more word 'faces', makes things easier, not harder. The child is now able to 'read'—in the sense that a person unable to understand music is able to play Chopsticks and God Save The Queen. He is able to read only what he has been taught specifically and we must face the danger that, like Chopsticks, a page of print may become merely something he knows off by heart; that he is practising the skill of recitation rather than of reading.

Again, the Sentence Method does encourage guessing.

It may initially tend to encourage inaccurate reading—
saying what it looks as though the picture ought to indicate
rather than trying to recognise friends amongst the row of
word faces below. Nevertheless despite all its shortcomings
it *does* encourage. It is full of interest. And it has complete
meaning. Its main disadvantage is so blatant that because it
stares us in the face we have so far overlooked it. Pictures are
so much more interesting than print that the child may
hardly bother with the words at all! And there is always the
chance that he is not looking at the word shapes as he says
their names, which slows up the process of linking picture
and word in his mind. However, there is a way of getting
round this difficulty that we shall examine in detail in another
chapter. Perhaps at this stage we should look into the
possibilities of the other main methods of teaching reading;
those concerned with parts of the word as opposed to its sum
total.

The original 'part' method is now seldom used, although
there are still a few country schools where it finds favour, yet
for hundreds of years 'c–a–t: CAT', the Alphabetic or
Spelling Method was used with enthusiasm. And this despite
the fact that the only meaning c–a–t can possibly have is
'See! A Tea'! (Or 'See a tee'.) The success of the method
was perhaps due to the stressing of the whole word shape
through concentrating on it letter by letter. Even in this
modern era we can still employ this principle in remedial
reading through a modified form of word building (see
Chapters 5 and 8).

The Syllabic Method evolved by Lancaster and Bell
followed the same lines. The emphasis was placed on the
syllabic parts of the word, but it was still spelt through, so as
to stress its individual letter sequence, which in the end
added up to its total character. Dickens poked fun at this in
Nicholas Nickleby, when Squeers explained the beginnings
of Activity Methods to Nicholas:

'B–O–T, bot; T–I–N, tin; bottin; N–E–Y, ney; BOTTINNEY, noun sustantive, a knowledge of plants. When he has learnt that Bottinney means a knowledge of plants he goes out and knows 'em.' Which meant that the unfortunate lad in question had to go out and get on with the weeding.

One of the main objections to Word Whole methods is that they provide no means of unlocking the meaning of words that have not previously been encountered, apart from the help provided by the sense of the context itself. Without a picture clue to help him the child is lost. And this is where the Phonic method comes in.

In the wake of Noah Webster's famous *Blue Backed Speller* followed the thought so obvious that for centuries it had been missed: that whilst C–A–T might not really result in CAT, the sounds that the letters stood for, when run together, could produce a sound picture in slow motion as it were, close enough to the word itself to enable recognition to take place. Ker-a-ter *did* add up to Cat. For a moment it seemed as though troubles and difficulties in the teaching of reading were at an end. And with any other language this might have been so.

English, however, is currently written in words composed of twenty-six characters which have their roots in the original Roman alphabet. Since the days of Rome we have as a nation been involved successfully or unsuccessfully in a series of struggles with other races which have left their mark not only on our racial structure but on our language.

The result of all this, as far as it concerns children learning to read, is that we have finished up with a language composed of parts of many tongues: Greek, Roman, Anglo-Saxon, Danish, French, Dutch, German, to mention only the main ones; but we continue to try to use an alphabet that is now totally inadequate to the written needs of our present bastard tongue.

Put more simply, this means that we have only the 26

letters of the traditional alphabet with which to represent the
40 or more sounds that occur in Modern English. No other
European tongue suffers from such an abominable handicap.

26 symbols trying to stand for more than 40 sounds might
still be made to work if their use was reasonably consistent,
but so often there is neither rhyme nor reason in the phonic
make-up (and therefore spelling) of English words.

Ker-a-ter—*cat*, a child discovers, or is shown, or is led
to believe. Then he finds this character *c* in another word:
mice. Only this time it has a different sound—the same sound
as the *s* in *mouse*! But this, he may think, is just one of those
exceptions to the rule teachers are always talking about. And
of course he is partially right. Only in English there are more
exceptions than examples of conformity. To go back for a
moment to *Jim* and *Jill*. The child 'reading' at this level
may after a time notice something similar about the two
'faces'. Ger-im—*Jim*; Ger-ill—*Jill*. The hook on the front
is a *Ger* sound. Ger-am—*jam*; easy! But then where is the
hook in *germ*? How is *get* pronounced? *Jet*?

Let us now try to follow the sound values of our Ker-a-ter
a little further, as a child trying to unlock new words with
the aid of phonetics may have to do.

Ker-a-ter—*cat*, her-a-ter (we are exaggerating the sounds
on paper in order to avoid using phonetic symbols—*her* is
taught, as we all know, as a breathy 'hhh')—*hat*. That is
regular enough. Wh-her-a-ter—*what*. Not 'wat' but 'wot'.
Yet *water* is not pronounced as 'watter', 'wotter' or 'waiter'
but as 'worter'! Yer-a-ker (or cer)—her-ter? Back to 'yot'!

Here is a simple word: *bow*. But it has two possible sounds
and a dozen different meanings. And the bow-and-arrow
sound interpretation can lead us into the deeper waters of
dough, doe, do, rough, ruff, through, threw, thorough,
cough, hiccough and the like, whilst the bow-down-to-the-
king sound goes off on a different track involving words like
bough, ought and fort—or fought.

Which is all possibly a little confusing; and therefore the best possible proof that we can have of the difficulties implicit in learning to read English as it stands at present. Sir James Pitman's Initial Teaching Alphabet of Augmented Roman employing 43 characters is, despite the initial prejudice which is the characteristic reaction to any projected advance in the field of education, winning over more and more supporters. At the time of writing, not one of the schools using i.t.a. has dropped out of the three-year-old experiment, but an increasing number are asking to be included. In view of the difficulties which any system of one symbol per sound must automatically remove, and further, in view of the quite remarkable success that has been experienced in the schools using i.t.a. (both conventionally and remedially) it seems more than probable that one day Sir James's system will be universally adopted. It can certainly be used by those of us with a working knowledge of it in conjunction with most of the specific approaches discussed in this book. But in view of the hundreds of years that the present clumsy, illogical and inadequate alphabet has managed to survive we would perhaps be unwise to forecast the date that something so patently valuable as i.t.a. will penetrate the fog of prejudice that conservatively-minded educationalists generate continuously by pouring cold water on red hot ideas. Perhaps they do it in self protection.

Until that jaundiced and prejudiced attitude disappears (and 'Experience' in teaching is all too often just another word for 'Prejudice') a high proportion of children will continue to experience difficulty with learning to read— over 40%. Of these, about half will manage to overcome their troubles, but some 20% will remain backward readers, retarded readers, or in the case of about two in every three hundred, illiterate. 20% of the population of this country is a lot of people.

In view of the stress which we have placed on some

knowledge of straightforward reading methods perhaps we should try to summarise the main points before moving into the remedial field.

Reading begins with pictures. Pictures that stimulate interest, curiosity, imagination—and the *spoken* word. Pictures that children will talk about, so that they become really familiar with the sounds and meanings of words that later on they will encounter in print. Pictures cut out of magazines, advertisements, papers and comics. Pictures provided with reading schemes. And best of all pictures painted, crayoned or drawn by the children themselves. Lots and lots and lots of big, big pictures that will train eyes to seek, lips to speak and ears to hear.

Then pictures with words underneath. Whole words, because they have meaning. Words with long, distinctive shapes like *aeroplane* and *lorry* rather than our original and perhaps too similar *Jim* and *Jill*.

Pictures with sentences incorporating these single words. *The Aeroplane flies. See Jill's Lorry.* Matching words to pictures, sentences to pictures, words to sentences with the picture as a guide, and then without.

The first real reading books will still be 75% pictures. The same few words occur over and over again, and are gradually assimilated. A vague connection begins to form between letters and sounds, beginning with the initial letters of words which are a little less given to treachery than those tucked away inside. The shape of individual word 'pictures' is clarified through copying, tracing, writing and playing with letters.

At this stage the child seems to be chanting rather than reading. And then, suddenly—Click! the whole complicated process falls into place and the child is truly reading. The miracle has happened.

Now as we shall see in the following chapter, all this will normally happen somewhere between four and seven. Even earlier if the child is exceptionally bright. But if it has not happened by seven we can throw most of the material in use out of the window and think again. If it has not happened by eight we can throw all the material out of the window; the child will have been conditioned by failure to shy at the very thought of infant primers—and what eight or nine year old is interested in pussies, bunnies and Baby Jane? This sort of thing merely serves to underline his growing feelings of inadequacy and inferiority.

Successful reading, then, involves:

R eadiness.

E njoyment.

A ge, ability, aptitude and attitude.

D iscussions.

I llustrations.

N euro-muscular skills.

G raded and suitable material.

Freddy

Chapter 2

Backwardness, Retardation: Past and Present Principles

"Boys and girls have their oddities just as much as do words."—
Sir Cyril Burt: Preface to *To Bee or not To Be*

To begin with, let us clear up this difference between 'Backward' and 'Retarded' readers. Backward readers are below the reading standard associated with their chronological age primarily through the handicap imposed by lower intelligence. Learning to read effectively does demand a minimum amount of intelligence. We may put this around I.Q. 55 to 60, although a number of gifted teachers will claim to have taught children of lower I.Q. to read. What is interesting to consider in these cases is whether or not the teacher has in fact raised the child's effective I.Q. to this minimal level as the result of the positive personal contact involved. If we believe in a child's ability, then our belief may liberate just that little extra bit of potential from the constraint of unsureness and inferiority holding him back.

But given that there is a lower limit, then obviously as that limit is approached reading will prove more and more difficult. A degree of backwardness in reading must be expected and accepted in children of below average intelligence. Does it matter if they are backward, at the moment, provided that at some future time they *are* going to read and equally important, that they are going to *enjoy* reading? What really matters is not how quickly they reach literacy, but that they *do* reach literacy.

A point we might note in this connection is that children of lower intelligence should not be forced to attempt formal reading in the Infant school, or even in the lower forms of the Junior school. If they are made to try before they are ready, and Reading Readiness will be discussed in detail later on, they will fail, and failure is a major contributory cause in nearly every case of trouble or difficulty with reading. Failure begets failure and makes success increasingly difficult to attain. Failure breeds a dozen undesirable emotional by-products. It can, as we have seen, inhibit the output of intelligence, which is why we are in part considering its effects under the heading of backwardness.

Conversely, positive feelings like success can work the other way round. Manifest intelligence is a mysterious thing which can and does improve in the right sort of environment. Happiness, success, a sense of purpose, self-respect, plus a feeling of well-at-least-my-teacher-likes-me, all add up to security, and security *is* the right sort of environment.

This is the factor which is often responsible for the disconcerting jumps which that king of inconsistencies, the I.Q., is apt to make, and also the jumps made by the quality which matters a great deal more—to both teacher and employer: the degree to which a child chooses to make use of this alleged measure of brain power.

Retarded readers are children whose reading skills are below the norm associated with their chronological age for reasons other than low intelligence, notwithstanding that, as we have seen, there may be other reasons for this *apparent* lack of grey matter!

As far as retarded readers are concerned, our main task is to discover exactly what it is that is holding them back and

to remedy this. It may be that the retarded child has missed
a great deal of schooling, perhaps through illness or through
poor attendance. In addition to trying to compensate for
what he has missed in terms of learning, we shall want to
know, say, why he has been away so much, because poor
attendance may be indicative of trouble at home, or the
particular illness he has suffered may have left him with a
slight hearing or sight defect.

Defects of sight and/or hearing that are not sufficiently
marked to attract either our attention or that of the child's
parents can in some ways be more serious from an educational point of view than more obvious defects that demand
glasses or hearing aids. Children suffering from this kind
of minor physical disability have to spend a high proportion
of their mental energy on the actual physical act of seeing or
hearing what is going on around them: what the teacher is
saying or writing on the board, what particular letters are,
and what sounds they are supposed to represent. Conse-
quently they have a smaller proportion of mental power
available for the job in hand, the actual process of learning.
They are the ones who always seem to be saying: 'What did
you say?' 'I beg your pardon?'—the ones who are always that
much slower than the rest of the class in catching on, and in
giving us an answer; the ones we have to repeat our questions
for, with continuous demands to pay more attention.

Children who sit badly, who hold books too close to their
faces or screw up their eyes with apparent effort, who 'Can't
see the board' and who sometimes can't see what's staring
them in the face, apparently, may well be the ones with weak
sight. These difficulties of sight and hearing may engender
other causes of retardation. Defective speech, too, inevitably
hinders progress in a skill which hinges on the spoken word.
If work is so much of an effort, children may tend to give up
trying and relapse into daydreams or just playing about.
And then the mixture of lack of success, frustration and

apathy will begin to feed back upon itself in a vicious and ever-strengthening circle. Here are the children who should be sitting in the front desks of our classes rather than the ones who want watching, or the eager beaver, never-put-a-foot-wrong monitors.

There are plenty of other causes of retardation: textbook psychology troubles, like jealousy of younger brothers or sisters, or just not being loved or wanted; frequent changes of school, or, in these days of high staff turnover, frequent changes of teacher; tiredness due to stopping up too late, or Too Much Telly; more controversial causes, such as Word-blindness (discussed in Chapter 5) or High Frequency Deafness, which causes difficulty in hearing certain of the consonants; less glamorous causes, like unsuitable material, badly graded and illustrated. And, let's face it, even from time to time the wrong methods or, worse still, indifferent teaching.

In practical terms we are rarely justified in labelling a child as a backward or retarded reader. We should forget about these unhappy labels and concentrate on finding ways of helping these children forward at their own best pace, and making sure that they *do* reach literacy.

But the trouble is that many children of lesser ability are retarded as well. Few of the so-called mentally handicapped E.S.N. or dull children achieve anything like the standard of reading of which they are capable. According to Gertrude Keir, 60% of children under I.Q. 85 fail to work to capacity (*Adventures in Reading*—Teacher's Companion). Perhaps we accept their apparent limitations too easily.

The same applies to a number of children in the fringe zone of I.Q. 80-95 who have trouble with reading. Because we manage to get them to the point where, perhaps in a manner devoid of enthusiasm, expression and sometimes meaning, they can stagger like third-rate robots through a simple book or two, we feel we have done a good job. Yet the bulk of the adult illiterates in this country were at one stage able to do this sort of thing. The child who leaves school as a seriously backward reader is always in danger of regressing to near if not total illiteracy. We should not, therefore, consider a child as being able to read unless he can cope with material of the level of difficulty associated with nine-year-olds. And by this ugly little word *cope* we should imply *understand the meaning of*, which is after all the whole point of learning to read.

Now it will be abundantly clear from our consideration of teaching methods so far that no one approach can hope to supply a complete answer to the task of learning to read. There have been a number of attempts to find more effective ways of combating both general and particular difficulties, however, and we may find some of these worth looking at.

The current ten year experiment with i.t.a. at the University of London Institute of Education is of course an attempt to kill all the birds of reading difficulty with one stone. i.t.a. deserves—and, of course, has now had—complete books to do it justice, and there seems little doubt from the statistics available so far that here is an attempt with a high potential of success. But, as long as the English language as we know it continues to exert its stranglehold on schooling, we shall need to make provision in remedial terms for the special difficulties implicit in its construction.

What concerns us more directly here is the success that younger children learning to read have had with i.t.a. This adds weight to the growing belief that $6+$ as the minimum starting age for average children, something that has gone unquestioned for many years, could be wrong.

Let us suppose for a moment that it is wrong, and that a child of average ability can be introduced to reading via i.t.a. at 4. The important question that remains to be answered is how much of what the four-year-old learns to read will have meaning for him? How many of the words he encounters in printed form will he have used and found out about in the form of speech?

We may think that no child is ready for reading until he is sufficiently familiar with the use and meaning of the spoken forms of the words in his reading books. Failure peers into this paragraph to remind us of the penalties of jumping the Reading Readiness gun. A child of I.Q. 75 is not going to be ready to read until perhaps nine, and if by then he has been bludgeoned into accepting that he cannot read by continuous failure, he is unlikely to show the spontaneous interest in and curiosity about words that marks so unmistakably the point in time when children are ready to read.

i.t.a. may well prove a panacea for reading difficulties— if the Augmented Roman Alphabet completely replaces that which we use currently. Children may be ready to read earlier with i.t.a., but i.t.a. is still in the experimental stage. And, as this is a book on Practical Reading, we cannot afford to linger on 'ifs' and 'buts'. Perhaps it will pay us to continue to be conservative over this matter of Reading Readiness, and remember that a late start is a small price to pay for reaching reading in the end. Failure is a penalty out of all proportion to the possible gain.

Another new method which looks at the difficulty of sound representation is *Words in Colour*, a somewhat revolutionary approach devised by Dr. Gattegno, perhaps better known for his mathematical apparatus. Briefly, this method is a system of giving a series of 47 colours and colour-mixtures to sound families, in place of sound or letter names. The approach, we may feel, has a certain primitive appeal in that reading begins with a one colour/sound language from which a series of rhythmic 'words' are built up orally. Since these words have no meaning at all to the child, and since some of the real words on the colour charts would puzzle many a secondary school child, it is difficult to see what stimulus in terms of interest they can possibly have.

Whatever other criticisms may be levelled at the first specially written reading series in i.t.a.—the *Downing Readers*—at least they are beautifully illustrated and full of meaning. The *Words in Colour* books, on the other hand, resemble a series of Admiralty code books—without even the pictures of ships! However, in a particular situation, and with a particular child (possibly one whose strength is word-building, and who is a girl, since 6% of boys are colour-blind), *Words in Colour* may have something to offer as a stepping stone to literacy.

It is sometimes surprising to see how many 'modern' methods are rediscoveries of what fell into abeyance a century or so earlier! The idea behind i.t.a.—that is, one symbol for each sound in the language—is hundreds of years old. Yet up to the present it has never succeeded in winning recognition.

In 1899 one Nellie Dale was working on lines not so far removed from *Words in Colour*. The Dale system of 'Sounds in Colour' stressed families of sounds: vowels, consonants, voiced and devoiced sounds. This system was also broadly the basis of the late Edith Norrie's 'Composing Box', which she used with such success at the Word Blind Institute in Copenhagen.

Setting aside colour blindness, one of the main objections to the use of various colours in reading material is that this alters the sum total of the word's shape by emphasising certain letters. Some parts of the word are heavily accentuated through the attraction to the eye which stronger colours possess; others are diminished by appearing in weaker tints. The result is that the 'face' by which ultimately a word is to be recognised can change. If we write *brand*, for instance, in a variety of coloured letters, any one of half a dozen words (e.g. band, bad, ran, and) can spring into prominence with disconcerting—or even embarrassing[1]—results. We need to

---

[1] Write the first three letters in one colour. . . .

think quite carefully about the disadvantages of using distracting, and in this sense, distorting, additions like coloured letters.

Dr. Stott's *Programmed Reading Kit* is yet another modern development of the discovery that words are made up of sounds. This is a series of graded teaching aids consisting for the most part of phonic games and apparatus. Like most phonic material, the actual words used are not wildly exciting; there is an element of the old 'cat sat on the mat' about the context. But the activities involved do two very worthwhile things. They provide logical help at what Dr. Stott calls 'the sticking points' in reading. And they actively and happily involve the children in the vital process of finding out about sounds and words for themselves. We may conclude a little later on that children will derive much more benefit from making apparatus themselves, and being in contact with the words involved right from the beginning.

The programme offered by Dr. Parker's S.R.A. Reading Laboratories is far more extensive. This concentrates on comprehension from the word go, which is to be commended. But the scheme is so large as to raise physical problems of accommodation in crowded classrooms.

One way round the phonic foolhardiness of our language is to restrict the words used in reading books to those which are phonetically regular until children have a secure foothold in this treacherous world of English words. This is what Daniels and Diack set out to do by way of the 'Phonic-Word' method in their *Royal Road Readers*. Such an approach is bound to place limits on the material that children may wish to use in making their own reading books, captioning their own pictures, and so on. Before the coming of i.t.a., the Phonic-Word method might have been assessed as a possible short-term (though from the child's point of view, a shortsighted), makeshift answer to the inconsistencies of our language. But again we may find that it still has something

c

to offer children who are either weak as regards visual memory, or who need additional but meaningful phonic practice.

The Kinaesthetic approach, a remedial method which might be subtitled 'Teaching by Touch', has proved itself to be very effective in cases where all else has failed. This was developed by Grace Fernald in the early twenties, during her pioneer work in the field of Word-blindness. But she adapted it from a principle that had been utilised many hundreds of years before. During the first century A.D., Quintilian wrote of tracing and feeling letters, whilst Andrew Bell, of Monitorial System fame, advocated writing with the finger in a tray of sand (primarily, we are forced to admit, because this was the cheapest way of writing, but also because the children learnt through feeling the word, as well as seeing and hearing it).

The Kinaesthetic method harnesses the motor sense, or the sense of feeling or sensation in movement, to those of sight and hearing. The original approach consists in essence of tracing word shapes in the air, but any form of modelling, cutting, moulding, painting or tracing letters on paper is an example of 'Kinaesthetic Reinforcement' at work. Indeed, every time a child writes a word down, he is reinforcing his knowledge of it in this way.

Fingering words composed of letters cut out of sandpaper or rough cloth, tracing over words that have been pricked with a pin so as to raise the surface of the letters, finger painting words in a mixture of poster paint and starch, and printing with letters carved on half potatoes are further practical examples of kinaesthetic help. Additional ways of obtaining Kinaesthetic Reinforcement are described in detail in Chapter 5.

Nearly all the approaches we have looked at so far have been concerned with parts of words, sounds, sound values, letters and colours. This is hardly surprising, since what a child lacking both success and confidence asks for is a *system* by which he may learn this unhappy subject called 'reading'. With things as they stand, as we have already said, there can be no complete and foolproof system. But, in one way and another, various people have attempted compromises even though, in terms of phonic values, two and two make four on this page, but eight, or sixteen or a hundred and five on the next. Letters, unlike figures, have no fixed values.

A further drawback is that sounds and bits of words cannot hope to appeal to the child in the same way as complete words or, better still, sentences. Meaning is the one and only thing that makes reading interesting at all!

But there are a great number of words which may or may not be met again in the early stages of reading, and a completely random selection is hardly likely to succeed. Many reading schemes are based on a 'Word Count' and try to use the words that occur most frequently in reading matter generally. The Ladybird *Key Words Reading Scheme* is an example of what can be done in this way, and another variation on this approach, designed for children who have more aptitude for number than language as such, is set out in Chapter 8.

The Word Count approach, like all the others, has definite limits. In this instance the snag is that the commonest words like *is*, *it*, *in* and *the* are difficult to illustrate on their own. Progress, it is true, will be accelerated once such words are known, but this is generally achieved by linking them to the rather less common but more interesting nouns that children want to read about.

For those of us who are already weary with theory, one practical way of teaching less able children, even non-readers, to read one-third of pretty well any book in the school (and by virtue of this fact the approach becomes a magnificent confidence-builder-cum-confidence-trick) is to get them to memorise the following:

Common Word Verse

> is it in the big one?
> for all of you said so!
> was he and I that can to fly?
> but come on, have a go!

Write it, recite it, trace it and read it. That is all the
children have to do. Then they count the words they can
recognise on odd pages of reading books, comics or anything
else to see if this one-third business is right. For the sake of
peace and quiet, it may be safer to say one-quarter! In the
process of recognising and writing down words in order to
count them, a great deal of useful repetition is taking place.
Add a few nouns through look-and-say and we may have
started a non-reader on the way to literacy.

Even with this simple approach, phonics will have to
follow, that dreadful-sounding kinaesthetic reinforcement
will have to be worked in, and so on and so on. We need to
make use of every resource we have. Mixed Methods, the
more mixed the better, are the most satisfactory. Let us end
this chapter, then, with a restatement of our conclusions so
far.

Principles of approach to less able readers

Helping children with reading is fundamentally a matter of
helping *children*. Techniques are secondary considerations.

FACT ONE: It is primarily people, not techniques, that lay the
foundations of success in reading. Therefore:

STEP ONE: We need to know our children, to make friends
with them and to share their interests.

In order to help a child with reading, it is necessary to
have some understanding of the technical problems facing

him. Adults, with their wide background of language experience, may not find it easy to accept that the skill of extracting meaning from groups of squiggles called words can be troublesome or difficult. Nevertheless, this is so. Glancing through a book in Russian or Chinese will help us to appreciate the position of the child unable to make sense of a single word. English, with only 26 letters to represent its 44-plus sounds, is in fact less logical in this respect than Russian!

FACT TWO: Quite a high proportion of children experience difficulty in learning to read simply because of the illogicality of the English language. Therefore:

STEP TWO: We must avoid an any-fool-can-read attitude, and accept that reading can be a headache and a heartache to many children through no fault of their own, even if we were among the lucky ones who 'just picked it up'.

Children with reading difficulties often feel that they are letting parents, teachers and themselves down. They may demand attention, or they may be self-effacing and nervous. Both groups seek reassurance; they need to feel they are loved, wanted, accepted and respected no less in spite of their lack of progress.

FACT THREE: Negative feelings—a lack of confidence, a sense of shame, of inferiority, frustration or failure—can in themselves form an effective block to reading progress. Therefore:

STEP THREE: We need to show tolerance, sympathy and affection towards the child; to build up his self-confidence by reference to successes in other directions; for example, in P.E., drawing, painting and craft.

A certain minimum level of general maturity is necessary before a child is ready—and therefore able—to acquire reading skills. The chronological age at which this will be achieved will vary considerably. Whilst bright, confident children may be ready for reading at four or even earlier, the average child will not be ready to start until five or six. Less able children, 'late developers', and those who are immature generally, may not be ripe for reading until eight or nine. We must not blame them for a condition over which they have no control.

Reading maturity can often be gauged from a child's use of, and response to, the spoken word. Can he understand and carry out simple directions? Can he listen to a story and repeat the gist of it in his own words? Can he recognise everyday objects in a picture and talk about them? Has he grasped the idea that picture stories run from left to right? Does he enjoy rhymes (that is, can he detect differences and similarities in sounds)? Can he do likewise with shapes? Can he recognise a few letters? And, above all, is he curious about 'what the words say'? Does he show unmistakable signs of *wanting* to read?

Children who are not yet ready for reading should be given plenty of Reading Readiness material: picture books, comics, painting and drawing books, tracing books, cut-out and stick-in books, musical toys, simple jigsaws and sorting puzzles; as well as opportunities to listen to stories, to act, to play with puppets, and to talk about their day-to-day experiences.

FACT FOUR: Until a child is familiar with the use and meaning of words in their spoken form, he will not be likely to succeed with the printed symbols that represent them in books. Therefore:

STEP FOUR: We must make sure that the child is ready for reading before urging him forward. Starting too early is a common cause of failure.

Children tend to take on the attitudes of adults near to

them, particularly of parents and teachers. A child who rarely, if ever, sees a grown-up reading a book for enjoyment is less likely to form a connection between reading and pleasure in his mind.

FACT FIVE: A child must not only be ready for reading, he must *want* to read. He must see some point in acquiring this skill. Therefore:

STEP FIVE: Let the children see that we derive a tremendous amount of pleasure and information from books. We should read them bits from books and newspapers and magazines that will intrigue them, and discuss the pictures in their own books and comics.

Reading concerns speech, sight and hearing, as well as intellect.

FACT SIX: A 10% deficiency in sight or hearing may, if undetected, cause as much as a 50% increase in the degree of difficulty encountered in learning to read. Therefore:

STEP SIX: In cases of failure, begin at the beginning. If a child wants to read, seems ready to read, but is failing to read, look out for weaknesses or defects in speech, sight or hearing. In cases of doubt, call in the school doctor.

The continuing effects of failure, the 'negative feelings' referred to in Fact Three, are firstly an acceptance of failure. The child decides that reading is something beyond him and stops trying. Secondly, he rejects further efforts to help him, together with reading books, as painful pointers to his inadequacy. He does not want to be reminded of his failure, and to be forced to try yet again what he knows from past experience he cannot do. He dreads the humiliation and exasperation associated with continual failure and will often go to some lengths to get away from reading, the classroom and even the school.

In such circumstances, continuing to toil at some 'dreary' reader until the first pages—and only the first pages—are known by heart is worse than useless, particularly if the book is intended for younger children.

FACT SEVEN: The conventional reading books, long familiar, are now no more than proof to the child that he is a non-reader. Therefore:

STEP SEVEN: Dispense with the conventional reading books completely, and with any other material that can only remind the child of past failure.

What is needed is some way of proving to the child that he can read—a way that is unrelated to conventional books, has a high degree of novelty and interest, uses a limited number of words that are suited to his chronological age, yet makes provision for these words to be encountered over and over again in different contexts. *The ultimate aim remains to increase the child's capital of confidence to the point where it will sustain reading skill.*

Whole words, and still more so, sentences, are complete in meaning, just as are spoken words and sentences. These 'whole-word' approaches are therefore the most meaningful and interesting ways of approaching the reading skills. Sound analysis in the early stages tends, in any case, to undermine rather than to build up this vital factor of confidence.

We should set out, therefore, to help the child to absorb thirty or forty whole words or brief sentences through any of the methods, apparatus or games described in later chapters, with the dual aim of providing a foundation on which he can build, and of bringing about a change in his attitude towards reading.

FACT EIGHT: Novelty of approach and concentration on a few

words suited to the child's age and interests will reorientate his feelings towards reading. Therefore:

STEP EIGHT: In place of books, we should employ novel games and apparatus involving whole words (and short sentences).

Children, like adults, tend to be more interested in themselves and their own doings than in anyone or anything else! The first reading books should be constructed by the child himself from material he has mastered through games and apparatus, or that he has collected in the form of labels, slogans, etc. The Common Word Verse is helpful, at this point.

FACT NINE: Reading and writing skills go hand in hand and reinforce each other. Therefore:

STEP NINE: Introduce a Personal Work Book (see Chapter 10).

At this stage the child should have a sight vocabulary of perhaps fifty to sixty words. He should be able to read his personal work books fluently, and a subtle change in his attitude towards reading should be apparent.

Nevertheless, the point is approaching when the child will need some means of at least being able to make an attempt at a new or unrecognised word. Additionally, there are some children whose basic weakness is visual memory; who are much stronger in aural memory[1] and who therefore will progress faster with phonic help.

Phonics, however, comes dangerously close to the Teaching

[1] A simple test to determine which is dominant is to ask a child to think of or imagine such things as: (a) a train; (b) the Beatles (or whichever group is in the Top Twenty at the time); (c) a motor bike; (d) a man chopping wood; (e) rain. Those with dominantly visual recall will tend to 'see' these things, whilst those who are dominantly aural (and thus more likely to derive help from phonic methods) will tend to 'hear' them.

of Reading, something that goes on in the Infant school and which we have been at pains to avoid. The phonic work that we will now begin to blend with other activities needs therefore to be just as carefully disguised.

FACT TEN: There is a limit to the amount of reading progress that can be made by word-whole methods. Therefore:

STEP TEN: We need to introduce the elements of phonics, but in an equally indirect manner through games and apparatus.

Shortly the child may be ready—and willing—to go back once more to the printed page. The books that he attempts will need to be very different in content and layout from anything he has failed with before (see Chapter 10).

As we lead the child towards this ultimate step in remedial work, we have to remember that his new-found reading confidence is at once the most important and the most delicate of his possessions. We must not let him go forward too quickly and risk failure.

We should allow him to continue with reading games involving additional words and sentences, and encourage him to make most of the material himself. Creative writing, especially in the form of personal work books, diaries and news, should play an increasing part in his allied activities. Comprehension work needs to be introduced as early as possible, too.

FACT ELEVEN: As the child consolidates his small reading vocabulary and his confidence begins to grow, the time will come for him to return to books. Therefore:

STEP ELEVEN: When, and only when, the child has acquired a sufficient sight vocabulary to guarantee success, a fresh start should be made with suitable series of remedial 'readers'. He will need to continue for a while with games and apparatus.

Reading for meaning should be stressed and tested, but the essential point to bear in mind is that support, encouragement and praise will take him further than techniques. In other words, we are back where we started, at

FACT ONE: It is primarily *you*, not your techniques or my techniques, that will lay the foundations of success in reading.

BIBLIOGRAPHY for this chapter

i.t.a. (Augmented Roman):
The Initial Teaching Alphabet, J. Downing (Cassell, 1964)
The i.t.a. Reading Experiment, J. Downing (Evans, 1964)

Words in Colour:
Notes, C. Gattegno (Educational Explorers Ltd., 1962)

Sounds in Colour:
On the Teaching of Reading, N. Dale (1899)
Success and Failure in Learning to Read, Notes by R. Morris, pp. 45-52 (Oldbourne Press, 1963)

Programmed Reading Kit:
Manual for the Programmed Reading Kit, D. H. Stott (Holmes, 1962)
S.R.A. Reading Laboratories Handbook, D. Parker (Nelson, 1963)

The Phonic-Word Method:
Royal Road Readers, Teachers' Book, Hunter & Diack (Chatto & Windus, 1954)

The Kinaesthetic Method:
Remedial Techniques in Basic School Subjects, Grace M. Fernald (McGraw-Hill, 1943)

Word Count:
Key Words Reading Scheme, W. Murray (Ladybird Books, 1964)

Chapter 3

The Visual-Verbal (V-V) Method

"The majority of E.S.N. children appear to be visually ready for reading before they are auditorily ready. It is therefore suggested that in the early stages a visual method should be used; that is, the beginnings of reading should concentrate on the acquisition of a sight vocabulary of meaningful words."—Tansley & Gulliford: *The Education of Slow-Learning Children*

The story of the birth of Look-and-Say or Word-Whole method is a delightful (and American) one.

It seems that a rather eccentric young teacher called Webb sat reading a broadsheet in the drowsy heat of a summer's afternoon towards the end of the last century. He sat, as it happened, outside the back porch of a farm where a cow was being milked.

One of his young pupils, a little girl of five, saw him there. She climbed into his lap in order to distract his attention from the paper, and began talking to him.

Suddenly Webb noticed the word *cow* on the broadsheet. A flash of inspiration crossed his eccentric mind, and he took the little girl's finger and placed it under the word. With his other hand he indicated the cow being milked nearby.

The girl looked at the cow, looked at the word and, so

goes the story, shouted, "Cow! Cow! I know what it says! I know what it says!" Look-and-Say had been born.

But is it not true that Comenius wrote a book called *Orbis Pictus*, the World in Pictures, some two hundred years earlier, with the same end in view?

Whatever the truth may be, Look-and-Say is perhaps the most important initial method of teaching reading that we have, and we are greatly indebted to whoever first saw the possibilities of such a system. But, if we look a little more closely at the lines on which it works, we shall see that in many ways it leaves a great deal to be desired.

Look-and-Say is based on the principle of association. An unknown visual symbol, the word, comes to be associated in terms of meaning with a known visual symbol, the picture. Research has shown that a new word has to be encountered twenty or thirty times under these conditions before sufficient meaning and familiarity has rubbed off to enable its 'face' to be recognised on its own. This, of course, implies real familiarity with the word shape and letter sequence as distinct from the superficial recognition necessary to be able to tell one word from another in the sense that a non-reader might quickly distinguish between Jim and Jill.

All the same, those of us with some experience in this field know only too well that many children can Look-and-Say away until they are black in the face, and will still fail to recognise given printed words on their own.

Now the supporters and followers of the Phonic camp will rush forward to point out that if only we would drop the foolish idea of tackling whole words and concentrate on putting them together sound by sound, such problems would not arise. But Phonic methods have even greater problems and difficulties surrounding them, as we have seen. Whatever else we do in remedial reading, we must try to preserve interest through meaning. *Yacht* has patently so much more

to offer in this way than a laborious process of 'yer-a-ker-
(?cer)-her-ter . . . '

To return to our original consideration of Look-and-Say,
the chief disadvantage of this method, as the Phonic-ites
will be crying out, appears to be that it encourages guessing.
This is true enough, but intelligent guessing prompted by
contextual clues and governed by the general content of a
picture is no bad thing. Unfortunately, it must be admitted
that, where the wrong guess is made, the resultant mislearning can be worse than no learning at all!

But to the chagrin of the Phonic-ites, we can point out
that the most serious disadvantage of Look-and-Say seems
to have been overlooked: that it can all too easily become
Look-and-Don't-Say; or Say-and-Don't-Look.

The fact of the matter is that when a child Looks at a
picture and decides what significance or meaning it has, he
may or may not look at the accompanying word or words as
he does the Saying part. The picture, after all, is so much
more interesting and meaningful, and therefore powerfully
attractive to the eye.

Now the principles of association demand that the two
things to be associated should be presented as near together as
is possible, both in terms of space and time. With Look-and-
Say, at best, there is always a brief interval during the
physical changeover from focusing on the picture to focusing
on the word. The two separate and completely different
visual symbols have to be linked by the sound of the word
name carried in the memory. At worst, if the child continues
to look at the picture as he says the word, he is doing no
more than stamping in an impression with which he is
already familiar. The point we should note at this juncture is
that there is no way at all of *ensuring* that the child does look
at the word!

Ideally, Look-and-Say would go one stage further and
become a Conditioned Response. This, as Pavlov demon-

strated, results from two stimuli being presented at *exactly* the same moment with the result that in quite a brief space of time either will automatically produce the same response.

Pavlov also demonstrated that the longer the interval of time that is allowed to elapse between the first stimulus and the second, the weaker the degree of conditioning. Here is the clue to the apparent ineffectuality of Look-and-Say in the case of so many children, and also to the large number of Look-and-Says necessary before learning—or conditioning—takes place.

From an ideal point of view, then:

(*a*) Word and picture should be viewed simultaneously.
(*b*) It should be physically impossible to look at the picture only.
(*c*) The emphasis, following on from (*b*), should be shifted from the known stimulus, the picture, to the unknown or less familiar stimulus, the word.

If all these conditions could be complied with, Look-and-Say would obviously become far more effective. The process of 'conditioning' the learner to respond with meaning to the new stimulus of the word would be achieved relatively quickly, without a great deal of conscious effort and with lasting effect. The original objection of guessing would not arise at all.

The concept of 'conditioning' children to read may cause some of us to wonder if a touch of 1984 is creeping in. But might we not agree that the hallmark of the skilled adult reader is his ability to react instantaneously to words or groups of words in terms of understanding, without the slightest conscious effort in terms of the mechanical elements of reading? He is thus able to concentrate his attention on what the words *mean*, not what sounds the groups of letters produce when decoded. The difference, put another way, is similar to that between the practised French scholar, who thinks *in* French, and the struggling tourist who has his work cut out to understand what is happening because he has to go through the mechanics of translation before he can arrive at meaning, and who therefore has to think *about* French.

The skilled adult reader, then, can no more look at a word and *not* read it than he can look at his face in a mirror and fail to recognise it. The ultimate in basic reading skill is that it shall become an automatic conditioned response, leaving the higher centres free to deal with the essence of communication: meaning. Given that this line of argument has aroused our interest, how many of us have been conscious of the fact that we have had to deal with the mechanics of reading in order to follow it? We might now be forgiven for adding a fourth aim in our idealised version of Look-and-Say, namely:

(*d*) The ultimate aim should be to reproduce as closely as possible the conditions for making the mechanical act of reading a given word into a conditioned response.

V-V, Visual-Verbal, is an extension of Look-and-Say that, to the horror of the Phonic-ites who have been nodding approvingly all this time, sets out to fulfil all these conditions, most of which appear on first consideration to be physically impossible.

The technical solution to the main problems of simultaneous presentation, prevention of picture only being looked at, and the shifting of emphasis from picture to word with a total resultant 'conditioning' effect is remarkably simple, as can be seen from the picture facing page 80.

A thickish piece of plain paper is folded in half, and a word, preferably a common word with plenty of interest and enough letters to give it a distinctive pattern, is printed boldly across the middle of the outside half. This word is repeated in smaller print well clear of the fold of the paper.

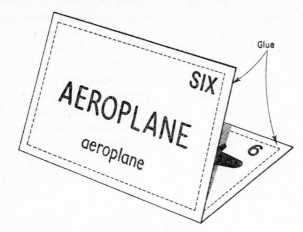

FIG. I. The Visual-Verbal basic card.

In the top right hand corner, well clear of either margin, a number name up to ten is printed (Fig. I).

We have used the word 'printed' deliberately in an attempt to keep the conventionalists at bay long enough at least to describe the exterior of the card. But undoubtedly they will have seen from the diagram that BLOCK CAPITALS are being used for the main word, and for the number name. 'In heavens name, why?' they will be exclaiming. 'Everyone knows that small letters with their tops and tails give each word its distinctive shape. Everyone with any teaching experience at all knows that!'

Experience, we pointed out in the previous chapter, can be another word for prejudice. But let us answer our critics.

It is true that projecting letters like *b*, *d*, *p* and *q* help form the features of a word 'face'. Unfortunately, from the point of view of the child learning to read, whose eye is as yet unsure as to which end of a letter or word it should look at for meaning, these same letters will happily give meaning,

D

but a totally changed meaning, when incorrectly attacked. This results in the reversal of words and letters commonly experienced in the early stages of reading. The word *dog* in the illustration can be misread as *bog*, *god*, *gob*, *bop* and goodness knows what else because of this factor.

Nearly all capital letters, on the other hand, present a bold, constant pattern which has no meaning when attacked incorrectly, and so does not present the eye with more than one possibility as to interpretation. Looked at from the wrong end, or put together in the mind in the wrong sequence, *b* can be interpreted as *d*, *p*, *q* or even a poorly formed script *a*. Its capital counterpart B is capable of no such four-faced action. DOG remains DOG whichever way we look at it[1].

The second reason that block capitals are employed is that word recognition takes place only partially as the result of the up-and-down letter outline. *What is of equal if not greater significance is the letter sequence.*

Let us consider the word *cat*. A short little shape with a *t* at the end to the eye of the *ab initio* reader who has to concern himself with these things. Now substitute the word *act*. Oh dear! Another short little shape with a *t* at the end. Yet *we* recognise each for what it is instantly, with no difficulty whatsoever.

We are conditioned to react not primarily to word shapes which may or may not be accurate guides to meaning, but to *letter sequences*. This is why we can recognise the word *reciept* in a flash as being *receipt*—but spelt incorrectly. The shape is virtually unaltered, but the letter sequence is not the one to which we are accustomed—or to which we have been conditioned—to react.

Since the prime difference between our two words *cat* and

[1] Large block capitals have been successfully used in America by Doman, Stevens and Orem in experiments concerned with teaching two-year-olds to read.

act is one of letter sequence there is everything to gain and nothing to lose by emphasising this sequence through the use of upper case characters. CAT and ACT provide more for the eye to get hold of, and therefore there is a better chance of the relative letter sequences being retained.

In this respect, V-V owes something to the bad old days when children had to spell out every word in order to learn to read. What that process of spelling did was to din in the letter sequences on which reading skill is partially based. Using block capitals achieves the same end more humanely.

For the Word-blind, capitals have even great significance, as will be described in Chapter 5 and, if our Doubting Thomases are still loath to agree with us, they had better turn to that part of the book and become still more confused. But, if they will bear with us just a little longer and keep an open mind, they may yet agree that there is possibly something in what we are trying to say.

Let us compromise by pointing out that, in any case, since the more usual form of the word appears in small print at the bottom of the card the reader has the best of both worlds. From the theoretical point of view, the word is there so that its shape can be linked to the meaning as read from the letter sequence of the capitals above.

The number merely signifies the moves to be taken in any race game where words, correctly read, entitle the player to move as would a dice. Children have much to gain through constructing their own games, writing out their own rules, etc., and details of specimen games are given in Chapters 4 and 8. But let us try to finish the description of our card.

On the face of the opposite, inside half sheet, a bold outline drawing illustrating the meaning of the word is so positioned that when the sheet is closed the picture lies directly behind the word on the front, yet cannot of course be seen. A bold figure representing whatever number name has been selected is similarly positioned behind the number

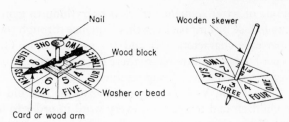

FIG. 2. Two ways to make a spinner. The numbers on the card may be in order, as on the first spinner, or haphazard, as on the second.

word. The folded sheet is then glued along its outside edges. This is a V-V Basic Card.

Children playing a reading race game will have a pile of up to ten cards which they try to read in turn. A child may either try to read the top card on the pile or use a spinner to select a number for him (Fig. 2).

Now let us examine what happens as the child tries to read his card. He has no choice but to look at the word with its bold and constant capital pattern as he tries to make up his mind as to what it might say. The weaker stimulus, not the stronger, is the one which is accentuated.

He may know the word, he may be unsure of it or he may have no idea at all as to what it signifies, but at least he is concentrating on the word pattern as such. He then 'brings the word to life' by holding it to the light, pressing it against a window pane, or by shining a bicycle lamp behind it, which understandably is always the most popular method.

Now, as he looks at the primary known stimulus, the picture, the secondary stimulus, the word which has to be associated with this, is still slap-bang in the middle of his line of sight. He was looking at this shape, he was aware of this stimulus, even if he was unable to read the word, as he picked the card up. He was still aware of the word at the critical moment when the meaning from the picture flashed into his mind, and he continued to look at the word, this time knowing for certain what it said, as he put it down. All the conditions we set out earlier in this chapter were being fulfilled.

The known stimulus, the picture, is always there as a clue, as a prompt, as a check or as a bit of fun, but never as an easier alternative route to meaning than that provided by the word. And, since the game is the all-important thing, the process of conditioning, takes place in an atmosphere which compares very favourably with that of the conventional reading lesson, which, to the backward reader, can resemble a mediaeval torture chamber.

Once the children grasp the idea behind these cards (the idea, not the ideology as set out in these pages!), they can begin to make their own, which of course will give them a head start in any game controlled by a proportion of their own cards.

A further development of the V-V principle is to arrange the cards in such a way that permutations of a limited number of common words will give more or less endless practice at a very low level of difficulty yet will maintain interest through the different contexts. This piece of apparatus, the V-V Multiple Reader, also introduces in an incidental fashion the beginnings of phonic awareness.

The V-V Multiple Reader consists basically of four 'packs' of rather smaller V-V Cards which are mounted on a spiral wire 'hinge' in such a way that different sentences may be built up by turning over the different cards (Fig. 3).

Whilst other children who have progressed a little further will enjoy (and benefit from) making Multiple Readers, it is probably better for us to make a specimen from which they can work.

Begin by folding ten quarto-sized sheets of paper in half, and marking them off in divisions, from left to right, as follows: $2''$; $2\frac{1}{4}''$; $2\frac{1}{4}''$; which should leave the right hand division measuring about $3\frac{1}{2}''$, Fig. 3(a).

Make this pack of larger divisions, into a set of V-V cards as previously described. Make sure that the words are written at exactly the same height from the bottom of each card—the main word in capitals $1\frac{1}{2}''$ from the bottom and the smaller script word $\frac{1}{2}''$ away. The numbers and number names may be left out, as in Fig. 3(b).

The actual words used can vary but, if we want those that occur most frequently in the remedial reading schemes that the child will later be using, the following are suggested:

AEROPLANES	CARS	TRACTORS	YACHTS	HOUSES
FIREWORKS	TRAINS	INDIANS	CANS	BOOKS

The plural forms are used in order to avoid repeating the word *a* which most children know. These plurals also lead to the discovery of the 's' sound as an introduction to the beginnings of phonic skills. '*Cans*' is included because very common words in this form can be legitimately taught on a Look-and-Say basis.

The first three 'packs' are now also made into V-V cards, bearing their words at the same $1\frac{1}{2}''$ and $\frac{1}{2}''$ heights, so as to make level sentences, Fig. 3(c). We must cheat a little in order to produce V-V cards from the commonest words like *saw* and *in*, but the means justifies the ends. We shall probably have to tell children what certain pictures are supposed to represent but, once we have told them, the 'clue' value will be strong enough to make the V-V principle work.

Words and 'clue' pictures will vary according to individual (and artistic) taste. The following have been used with success.

1st Pack	*2nd Pack*	*3rd Pack*	*4th Pack*
—	—	—	AEROPLANES

(The blank cards at the top of the first three packs mean that a child can begin using the apparatus by concentrating on the right-hand pack only. Once he knows these words, he can lift up the blank on the 3rd pack and work with two-word

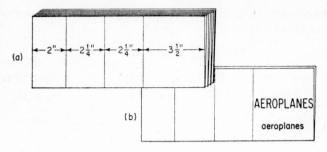

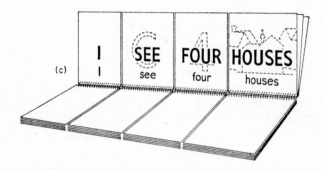

FIG. 3. The V-V Multiple Reader.

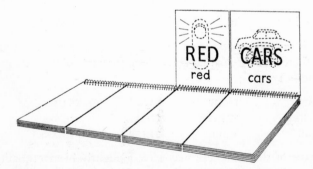

FIG. 4. The V-V Multiple Reader with the two right-hand packs only in use.

permutations (Fig. 4). When he is ready, he can bring in the other two packs.)

| BOYS | LIKE | RED | CARS |

('Colour' words are printed in the appropriate colours, as is the glowing 'traffic light' picture clue.)

| GIRLS | BUY | LITTLE | FIREWORKS |
| I | SEE | BLACK | TRACTORS |

('C'—as the 2nd illustration—may be regarded as slightly misleading, but remember that we are only trying to provide clues to the printed forms of words.)

| YOU | SAW | GREEN | YACHTS |

(*Saw*, like *can*, is a very common word that needs to be known as early as possible. Both words have more than one meaning, but the picture clue will trigger off the sound of the word. Then the child has to consider the context and arrive at the particular significance which his common sense tells him applies. In this way a child is led to think carefully about the *meaning* of what he is reading right from the start. He is making his own comprehension exercises.)

| THEY | HAVE | BIG | CANS |
| IS IT | IN | THE | BOOKS |

(*Is it in* . . . can be used to take phonic awareness a stage further, if children are asked to look for particular letters and sounds.)

AND	DRAW	TWO	TRAINS
THEY	PAINT	FOUR	HOUSES
ME	MAKE	THESE	INDIANS

(Some of the sentences may have a slightly bizarre quality, or may not make very good sense. This, in practice, adds to the appeal of the work as far as children are concerned, and

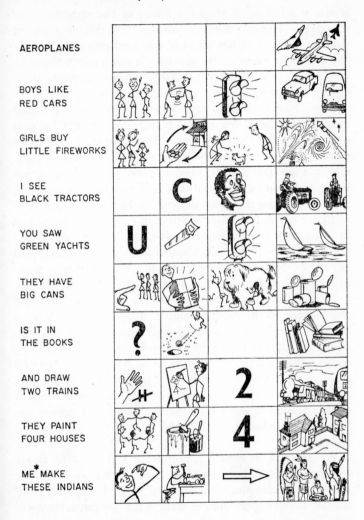

FIG. 5. Some specimen clues for the V-V Multiple Reader. "I" and "THE" can generally be taken as known.

* In the bottom row, "WE" can be substituted for "ME".

it is a good thing if they are aware of the importance of meaning—comprehension—from the start. When using *me* (last line) the child has a test of accepted grammar as well. We can allow *me* when the sentence is one 'spoken about/by an Indian' primarily because *me* is such a common word. Or we can purse our lips and substitute *we* for *me*.

Some specimen clues are shown in Fig. 5. We admit quite freely that a few of our picture clues might be misunderstood, and that they look a little like excerpts from a comic strip—but from the child's point of view this is actually in their favour. We need material that he will enjoy using and reading, material that is intriguing and amusing, and that will not prove too difficult for him to make for himself later on. A few minutes spent in suggesting the sort of drawings that may be expected as clues for half a dozen less obvious words (using blackboard and coloured chalk) will effectively prevent misinterpretation. Alternatively, a more experienced reader can act as a guide during the initial stages.

All that has to be done now is to punch small holes along the bottom of the cards, about $\frac{1}{4}''$ from the edge, and to thread a spiral of thin wire through them, so as to hold the whole together once the individual cards are separated by cutting down the pencil dividing lines. A spiral wire from an old loose-leaf notebook may be used, or, better still, the spring spines from old school calendars. An uncut sheet of card is needed to strengthen the back, and the edges of the four sections should be trimmed so that they do not foul each other.

We are not, in conclusion, putting V-V forward as set apparatus, but rather as an advanced, logical and effective *method* of helping reading forward with the advantage of actively involving children in making the apparatus they will use.

We have no theoretical axe to grind or torch to carry. We have no intention at present of making V-V into a commercial venture when, as we have pointed out, the use of ready made material might rob the child of some of its value. We would like parents as well as teachers to share the possibilities of our approach, and to adapt it as they think fit.

Again, let us stress the folly of putting all our teaching eggs in one basket. There is no one method. But V-V plus i.t.a. plus confidence might prove an attractive formula for the concrete material of which the foundations of success mentioned earlier on are made.

Chapter 4

V-V Tug o' War

"Skill is born of delight."—Sir K. Clarke

We have already considered the contribution which reading games and converted conventional games can make in changing the attitude of the non-reader through providing a 'play' activity in place of the possibly hated and feared 'reading lesson'. We will continue further with this theme in Chapter 8. From our immediate point of view, however, we are equally concerned with what is literally a confidence trick; bolstering the non-reader's confidence by involving him in a game that turns on the reading of V-V cards, and then suddenly pointing this fact out to him. 'Of course you can read, Robert,' we say. 'You've been playing that reading game half the morning! Now write some of those words you know in your Work Book.' And Robert thinks to himself: 'Well I suppose I must be able to read after all. And it isn't really as hard as I thought; not when I'm playing those games.'

Now, whilst it is simple enough to think up complicated reading games with instructions printed all over the place, it is not quite so easy to devise a game that is suitable for the child who can hardly read his own name; one that involves

half a dozen words or less to begin with, yet has all the satisfaction, interest and competitive attraction of the more
sophisticated reading activities.

V-V Tug o' War has proved to be a winner even for the
loser in this respect. It can be played by two non-readers,
or by small teams. It is a game that the children can make
themselves, without difficulty, and it can be played quietly
whilst more able children are getting on with other work, a
point that will be appreciated by the teacher with the problem
of a couple of very backward readers in an otherwise reasonably bright class.

The children concerned are told that they are going to
make a special game, and asked to collect old toy soldiers,
plastic figures that have been gifts in cereal packets—any
model figures that can stand upright. Or of course they can
cut out and paint their own. These are arranged in two teams
as for a tug o' war, and a string 'rope' is attached to each,
either by tying or glueing.

The teams need a cardboard 'field' (see Fig. 6) on which
to compete, and this, after being painted green, is marked
out in three divisions (A, B and C) on either side of the centre
starting mark. Details like a bit of rag to represent a hand-
kerchief glued to the centre of the string, coloured rubber
bands for team markings and so on can be added as ingenuity
suggests.

The prospective players are then invited to collect some
words for use in the game. They may well bring along an
advertisement of perhaps the only word they can recognise,
and if this is a brand name—*Cadbury's* or *Raleigh*, for
instance—we can accept this, adding the name of the article,
so that the V-V card reads: CADBURY'S CHOCOLATE, RALEIGH
BICYCLE, etc. The important thing about these first words in
this situation is that above all they have meaning and interest
for the children.

Chocolate and *bicycle* may seem odd words to use as a new

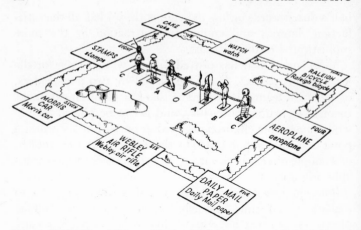

FIG. 6. V-V Tug o' War, with the field, figures, and V-V cards set out ready for play.

beginning in reading, but are they? They are long words, much longer than *pussy* and *baby*. But they have distinctive outlines and letter sequences and they are not as easily confused as shorter words or, worse still, a set of words like *cat*, *sat*, *hat*, *bat*, *fat* and the rest of that odd phonic family. These older children have left the world of *pussy* and *baby* behind. *Chocolate* and *bicycle* are words that can be seen and heard at all levels of reading and speaking. They are not babyish words that smack of the Infant school atmosphere and scream, 'Look at this child! He can't even read itsy-bitsy words and he's EIGHT—or TEN—or IN HIS T-E-E-N-S!'

If we write the selected words on the board in block capitals and script, the children can start making the necessary V-V cards themselves. They may well learn or half-learn these word 'faces' as the result of the concentration on shape, the interest, the kinaesthetic help of copying, and the repetition that follows in the wake of 'Oh-dear-I've-gone-wrong-can-I-start-again?'

However, when the cards are finished, there will be at least one or two that each child knows, because he or she suggested them. The game can now be started.

The children set up their tug-o'-war teams on the field, and place all the V-V cards round the edge. For less than six words, a dice will be needed. For six to twelve words—and this is the maximum that should be used in any one session— a wooden or cardboard spinner will have to be made (the boys will enjoy using their initiative over this), to operate on a card 'clock' base numbered as shown in Fig. 2, p. 52.

After deciding which side should start by tossing up, the child who has won the toss throws the dice or spins the spinner. He then has to read the V-V card corresponding to the number indicated. Having made his attempt, he holds the card in question up to the light to check, and both he and his opponent look at word and picture together in order to ensure fair play. They are, of course, also learning the word if it happens to be one that either or both cannot recognise, through the conditioning effect of V-V previously discussed.

If the child is right, he is allowed to pull the teams one space towards his side of the field. It is now the second child's turn. Suppose, for the sake of argument, that he is unable to read the word selected by pointer or dice; he knows that if his opponent gets one more word right he will then be within one 'pull' of victory. And this makes him look very, very carefully at the word he has been unable to recognise, so that he will know it should luck favour him with that number next time. He is able to put all his effort into assimilating this word without the doubts, disinterest, and fears that normally complicate his efforts to read; because, for his part, he is no longer concerned with words but with winning a game. And whether he wins or whether he loses, he will be building up that vital initial sight vocabulary that will prove to him that he can read, and enable him to go on to harder material.

It might be objected that a child could just *remember* that Card 4 on the right hand side is AEROPLANE. But when at

last fate is kind and gives him Card 4 to read, he triumph-
antly announces it as 'aeroplane'—whilst looking at the
word! And he still picks up the card to check. He has perhaps
spent more time on learning the word shape as he kept
glancing at it throughout the game than anyone else who
wasn't too sure what the card said.

Once all the words are known, the children will complain
that nobody can win. They then get down to making a fresh
set, or to enlarging the basic V-V cards into basic sentence
cards by adding, perhaps, *Here is a* . . . . illustrated by an
arrow, and *Look at the* . . . . illustrated by spectacles. But by
this time the non-readers will be non-readers no longer, and
itching to have a go at the more complicated race games,
where large packs (20–40) V-V cards are in use.

Chapter 5

A Word for Word-blindness

"Able was I ere I saw Elba."

Whether or not such a thing as Word-blindness exists threatens to become as big a controversy as rages between Phonic-ites versus Look-and-Sayers. The fog of prejudice tends to make us mind-blind in evaluating the evidence presented.

'Of *course* no such thing exists in children, given that they have adequate vision. If a child can see everything else around him perfectly well, why should he be "blind" to the form of a word? Take Johnny Cantreed, for instance. He sees well enough to go to the pool, or to tell his dog from the dozens of others like it. Nothing the matter with his vision. Word-blind? Just lazy, if you ask me!' This is the sort of comment that we must expect to hear in many staffrooms.

Now it *is* true that a child with adequate vision is capable of seeing words in a book. But we have already concluded that there is much more to the skill of reading than that. A word has to be perceived correctly, and Word-blind children, it is thought, suffer from a particular form of reading disability which shows itself as faulty perception. Such children do see letters and words, but either fail to recognise them, or worse still, take them for what they are not.

E

Part of the reason for this is thought to be the non-emergence of cerebral dominance, with the result that difficulty is experienced in distinguishing between left and right.

Cross-laterality, which shows itself as a tendency, for example, to shut the right eye whilst aiming an imaginary gun (which means that the left eye is the dominant one), but to catch an imaginary ball in the right hand (right dominance) and then to kick at it with the left foot (left dominance) is also associated with Word-blindness.

Some caution is needed in evaluating the significance of cross-laterality in any given case, since a fair proportion of cross-laterals prove to be good readers. These are generally children with a *marked* preference for one eye or the other, which is less indicative of Word-blindness. But the 'crossed wires' effect of hand and eye in opposition does tend to increase the likelihood of reversals, and to weaken the kinaesthetic help normally obtained through writing, and so make the act of learning to read just that much harder.

For a child already at a disadvantage, therefore, in terms, say, of low intelligence, cross-laterality may prove to be a serious handicap. As far as Word-blindness is concerned, it is cross-laterality plus *uncertainty* as to dominance that should lead us to make further investigations.

Now this uncertainty as to direction is of little consequence when looking at objects: dogs, pools and what have you. But, in dealing with words and letters, the eye will be tempted to start looking for meaning from the wrong side or end, particularly (and this is quite often the case in English) when the printed symbol makes perfectly good sense—but the wrong sense—when so treated. Few sentences are as foolproof in this respect as the one which forms our quotation on page 65.

The pool is still a pool whichever way it is looked at. The dog is still a dog whether looked at from head or tail, or from the middle outwards. But these two words attacked from left to right result in *loop* and *god*. Reversing words in this fashion is of course a stage through which a fair number of children pass; the classic examples being *for* for *off*, *no* for *on* and *saw* for *was*. Individual letters, particularly *b* and *d*, are confused but, once the correct eye-movement from left to right becomes established, such errors rapidly disappear.

This is not so in cases of Word-blindness. Persistent reversals, and even the inversion of letters like *h* and *y*, *p* and *d* can be symptomatic not so much of lack of practice in correct attack as of faulty perception. This combines with an inability to grasp and retain the letter sequence patterns of words to give another characteristic symptom: extraordinary errors in spelling. Here is an actual example:

I twen no a syid.	*I was stol for thre syds.*
I went on a ship.	I saw lots of other ships.

There is evidence here of word and letter reversal and of letter inversion. In other cases, whole lines of writing, whether original or copied from a book, will be turned round the wrong way. An example of this 'mirror writing' in a seven year old of average intelligence is shown facing page 81. The lack of awareness of shape also comes out in his drawings of houses, one of which has windows (with the frames running the wrong way) and the other has a total absence of features, yet is crayoned over, signifying that to the child it is complete.

Children who make this sort of mistake in writing and whose oral reading attempts are persistently punctuated by reversals, by letter confusion and by the omission of words and the insertion of words that are not in the context, may well be suffering from the handicap we are discussing. There are other indications which may help us to be more certain about this. The handwriting itself may be unrhythmical, lacking in any one decided style, cramped and 'stuttery'.

Speech often develops much later than would be expected normally, and parents can give us helpful information in this direction, and also as regards illnesses in early childhood, Rubella during the mother's pregnancy, Rhesus incompatibility, a difficult birth or head injury during early infancy are also associated factors. Word-blindness tends to occur more frequently in ambidextrous and left-handed children than in those who are right-handed, and also in those who have residual defects of speech, but it is important to note that what we may term the 'secondary' symptoms may or may not be present in any one Word-blind child. The confusion as to direction and shape and the peculiar spelling are the primary signs (Fig. 7).

However, we are not suggesting that our colleagues in the classrooms and staffrooms (or classrooms used as staffrooms!) should go from one extreme to the other, and treat every child in their school who has difficulty with reading or who occasionally reads *saw* for *was* as Word-blind. The Ministry of Education, quite uncharacteristically, is less cautious. In an analysis of unusual causes of reading failure, it places Word-blindness (under the frightening title of Strephosymbolia) second only to Emotional Difficulties, with an incident of 32%. On the other hand, the Ministry of Health, it is even more interesting to note, categorically refuses to admit, like our quoted staffroom, that such a thing exists.

Now before we in the practical situation dismiss 32% as something of a statistician's hangover, let us remember that for every one classical case, which possibly accounts for less than $\frac{1}{2}$% of our children who cannot read, there are probably a dozen others whose symptoms are less clearly defined or masked and complicated by other factors such as the side-effects of Word-blindness: lack of confidence, feelings of inferiority and a general emotional turmoil. A low intelligence, slight defects of sight and/or hearing, unsuitable material or method and other more conventional reasons for

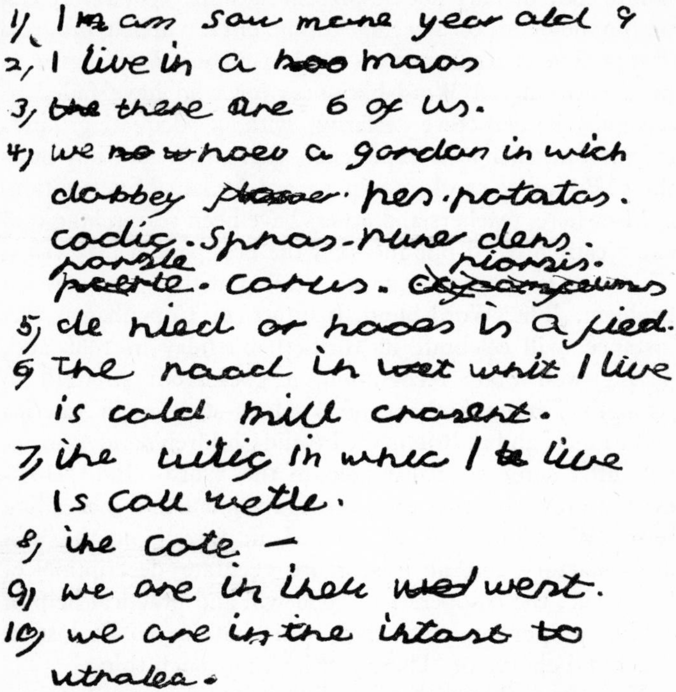

1. I am so many year old 9
2. I live in a house maos
3. there are 6 of us.
4. we have a gardan in wich
   dabbey has. pes. potatas.
   codic. Spras. nune dens.
   parsle.
   perte. corus. riorsis.
5. de nied or hooes is a pied.
6. The raad in wet writ I live
   is cold mill crasent.
7. ihe uileg in whec I te live
   Is call uetle.
8. ihe cote. —
9. we are in iheu med west.
10. we are is the intast to
    utralea.

FIG. 7. Characteristic symptoms of Dyslexia in the written work of an intelligent nine-year-old boy. Note: dabbey (daddy), codic (cabbage), dens (beans), de nied (behind), intast (continent). Note also letters omitted and put in for no apparent reason.

1. I am so many years old 9
2. I live in a house
3. There are 6 of us.
4. We have a garden in which daddy has potatoes, cabbage, sprouts, runner beans, parsley, carrots, parsnips.
5. Behind our house is a field.
6. The road in which I live is called Mill Crescent.
7. The village in which I live is called Westerleigh.
8. The east.
9. We are in the west.
10. We are in the continent of Australia.

failure may or may not be present as well. Very rarely can we pin the blame on any single thing, but it will help progress if experienced teachers who are fortunate enough never to have encountered Word-blindness (or who have failed to recognise it) will cease declaring, without adequate grounds apart from their own experience, that there isn't any such thing. Prejudice can be another word for lack of perception.

Elsewhere, teachers and others have been researching into and treating Word-blindness for the best part of fifty years. This is a long time to go on dealing with a non-existent problem. The Word-blind Institute in Copenhagen, for instance, will celebrate its thirtieth birthday in 1966 and, having won State recognition, it goes from strength to strength. There are other centres of long-standing in America and France, and in Britain the Invalid Children's Aid Association offer some specialist help to the Word-blind.[1] However, we may feel that until this unfortunate and misleading term 'Word-blind' is abandoned in favour of the still unsatisfactory but at least more accurate description of 'Dyslexia', the co-operation, good-will and practical help of a high proportion of teachers will continue to be lost in this blind chorus of 'There just isn't any such thing.'

Now, from the practical reading point of view, what is to be done if we are faced with the problem of a child who exhibits many of the strange symptoms listed above? He may prove to be intelligent and well adjusted, although how long an intelligent child can endure the frustration of failing to learn to read whilst his peers do so with ease and remain well adjusted is a nice point. What we are inferring is that poor emotional adjustment is not the prime cause of reading difficulty in these cases.

There would appear at present to be no way in which the presumed physical reasons for faulty perception can be

[1] James Webster opened the first Reading Clinic for Word-blindness in Britain in 1964.

treated. The lack of dominance may be caused by direct injury to the brain, through disease, through inherited characteristics or through a minute fissure in the parietal-occipital area responsible for speech and language. The end result is that neither hemisphere of the brain achieves dominance through the normal processes of maturation.

Our immediate problem, then, is to find some way of compensating for the weaknesses in perception through the direction of our teaching, and we shall therefore accentuate methods other than those concerned solely with whole words. Since reading is primarily a visual skill, however, we shall still have to train the eye in word and letter recognition, particularly as regards looking at print consistently from left to right.

What we shall do is to return to the out-dated, out-moded but possibly still valuable Alphabetic techniques as used by Quintilian nearly two thousand years ago. We shall employ solid plastic letters and cubes, and build up words from basic V-V cards that will act as unmistakable guides in the matter of initial word recognition so difficult for these children to accomplish.

Another alphabetical approach, and one that gives considerable scope for phonic practice as well, is based on a simple piece of apparatus called 'Sentence Squares'. To make such a set, we begin by cutting a length of $\frac{1}{2}''$ sq. wooden rod into $\frac{1}{2}''$ cubes, and we drill these through the centre so that they can be threaded on an elastic lace, Fig. 8(a) and (b).

The cubes carry letters on their faces as follows:

8 of A E I O	6 of B C S T	4 of K W V Y
6 of U A E I	6 of D F M T	2 of J Q X Z
6 of C P R H	6 of G H L N	4 blanks

The selection of letters is based on an analysis of letter frequency in the commonest words, but it can of course be varied. Letters can be painted, stencilled or drawn with a

felt pen; they can be typed on to a sheet of paper, cut out and
glued in place, or they can be cut out from suitably sized
newspaper and comic captions. This part of the construction
children can happily and profitably carry out for themselves.

An added refinement is the painting of the cubes so as to
draw attention to the difference between vowels and consonants. Green for consonants, yellow for vowels and red for
spaces is a pleasant combination, but again we—or the
children—can suit ourselves. All the actual letters should be
plain black.

The sentence squares material is used to construct words
by building them up, letter by letter, on the elastic lace.
When words or sentences are completed they will stay in
place if the end of the lace is wedged with a piece of match-
stick. This means that they can be moved around without
falling to pieces, one of the major frustrations of 'ordinary'
word building. It also means that by rotating different cubes
different words can be obtained, which accentuates the
sound quality of the various letters, Fig. 8(c). This is one of
the most interesting and, at the same time, effective ways of
teaching phonics, although Dyslexic children will also derive
benefit from the method outlined in Chapter 6.

The V-V cards used as guides for Sentence Square work
are in fact the best visual material to use with these children,
not so much because of their novelty which often makes the
Dyslexic feel that he is being offered something new (which
helps him basically because he believes it will!), and not even
because of their conditioned reflex action, but because of
their accentuation of correct letter sequence through the use
of capitals.

Capital letters, as detailed at length in Chapter 3, seldom
make sense if looked at from the wrong end or turned upside
down. There is much less temptation to reverse words if they
have no meaning when so treated. Something may be lost in

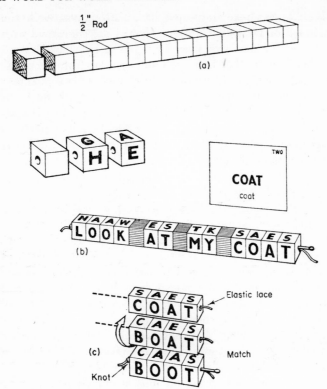

FIG. 8. Sentence Squares.

word shape when the bits that stick up and down are cut off, but it is the allegedly very helpful letters like *b*, *d*, *h*, *p*, *q* and *y* which cause most trouble to Dyslexic children. And capitals do have a very distinctive and characteristic outline all of their own; they are not so small and fiddly and, after all, we print most of our important notices in capitals in order that they should be read easily and correctly[1].

[1] Electric typewriters using upper case characters only are gaining popularity for the same reasons.

Phonics, as already indicated, have a strong position in the treatment of Dyslexic children. Phonics are concerned with parts rather than with wholes, and where the wholes are unreliable we shall do better to build them up from the parts. Once a Dyslexic child has seen the correct letter sequence a number of times, he is far more likely to read the word correctly when it occurs again. If his initial reading is concerned with material printed in capitals, he is less likely to keep on seeing wrong combinations of letters and confusing his concept of the word. Phonic work for older Dyslexic children, or for those who are just plain backward readers, need not be babyish either. *A for apple*, *B for Baby* and *C for Cat* (sometimes *C for Pussy*) should give way to the sort of material shown facing page 97. An old typewriter (and sometimes there is one hidden at the back of the Head's private store of rubbish) can be of tremendous help. There is the thrill and kudos of being allowed to use this machine, and the concentration on the letter sequences involved in forming words, letter by letter, looking at the BLOCK CAPITALS only because the keyboard shows only these.

As the typewriter will automatically print the smaller characters the correct way round, the Dyslexic child will see a 'translation', as it were, of what he is writing in capitals. There will be no danger of his mislearning shapes, as may sometimes occur through the kinaesthetic power of ordinary writing. As far as the physical act of writing is concerned, he is better off in the early stages tracing words rather than trying to copy them. The vital thing is to give him plenty of experience of and practice with the *correct* form of the word despite the worst his faulty powers of perception and attack can do.

As to the problem of reversals, so very marked in these cases, we may use little mnemonics like: *b* pushes the *b*arrow in front of him, but *d* *d*rags his after him; or, as in Dr. Stott's Reading Kit, *b* is like the bat hitting the ball, while *d* faces

FIG. 9. Some mnemonics to help to distinguish between b and d.

the same way as a picture of a duck shaped like a *d*. We can point out that *bed* cannot be written any other way, otherwise it does not look like a bed—the end supports would be in the wrong places if *b* and *d* were reversed (Fig. 9).

One way of attacking the root of this reversal difficulty is to force the eye to look at the correct end of the word or letter first by causing the word to pass across the line of sight from right to left. This is achieved in the Reading Clinic by mounting Sentence Squares (and, later on, 'reversible' words cut from old books) on the carriage tops of an electric train. The words are read through a slit in the top of a bootbox 'tunnel', the train running slowly in a clockwise direction. Few authorities are going to pay for this sort of equipment, however, and we must make do with more prosaic approaches like those detailed in Chapter 4. There are other and simpler ways of making words move: printing them on a pack of postcards, for instance, with each card bearing the same word or words in the same sized characters and at the same height, but a fraction to the left of its predecessor. 'Flicking'

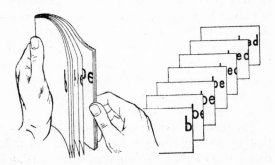

FIG. 10.

Fig. 11. The cardboard 'record' on the gramophone turn-table (*left*) and the turn-table covered by the cardboard box (*right*).

or 'fanning' the pack will produce the illusion of the word moving from right to left. The first few cards, of course, will bear only the first part of the word, as shown in Fig. 10.

Yet another mechanical way of producing this effect is to make cardboard 'records' of words and play them on an old gramophone turn-table (in a clockwise direction) so that the words can be read through a slit in a cardboard box which has replaced the lid of the gramophone (Fig. 11).

Of the intial reading games that are vital to the establishment of a basic sight vocabulary one that has particular relevance to Dyslexia is Parachuting.

Parachuting is simply Snakes and Ladders in reverse. Instead of starting at the bottom of the board, trying to get to the top and slithering back down the snakes, Parachuting is played by starting at the top left hand corner ('jumping out') and trying to land in the bottom right hand corner. Players stopping on squares touching aeroplane tails are 'caught in the slipstream' and blown back up to the line above. Those lucky enough to stop on a square touching the top of a parachute drop straight down to the square occupied by the figure at the 'chute's end.

The point of reversing the traditional journey upwards is that by moving along a line from left to right, and then continuing on the following line, again starting from the left

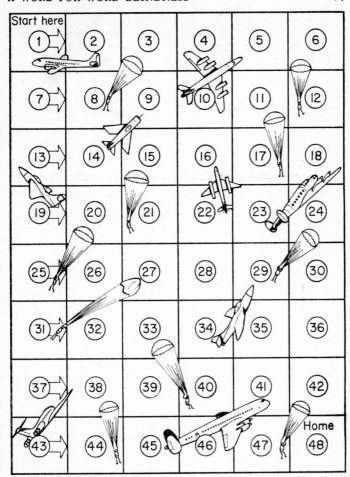

FIG. 12. Parachuting.

hand square, the child is reproducing, in slow motion, the movements his eyes must make when travelling along a line of print. He gets used to the idea that things have to go from left to right all the time.

Moves in the game are determined in the usual way with V-V basic cards, each child scoring the number indicated by a correct reading. An illustration of Parachuting, which can be drawn by children themselves, is shown in Fig. 12.

There is no quick cure for Dyslexia, but it is a disability or visual weakness that with understanding and continuous help may be overcome. Inevitably treatment is a long process, beginning with the child coming to realise that he does in fact have some sort of visual handicap which his teacher will work with him to defeat. Like all practical reading, it begins and ends with the child himself as a person, with the re-establishment of confidence in his ultimate ability to read.

Chapter 6

Rhythm, Movement and Drama
in Reading

"Teach by doing whenever you can, and only fall back upon words when such doing is out of the question."—Rousseau: *Emile*

We have now considered most of the theoretical considerations that, as was pointed out in Chapter 1, cannot very well be avoided if we are to know exactly where we are going—and why. Even so, our academic points, if such they must be called, have at least been practically related to method, and in this way we have tried to form some idea of the value and possible uses of Visual-Verbal material.

From now on we shall be able to concern ourselves completely with practical techniques of various kinds that have been found to work in the classroom, involving different applications of well-tried principles.

The first three of these are all based on the help which movement is known to give to learning. The simplest example of this 'kinaesthetic reinforcement' at work in reading is the value of tracing over words with a thick soft pencil or crayon. The kinaesthetic principle can be extended to help with phonic work, to bring words to life and to give children opportunities to move, act and relieve tension generally, as well as to enjoy meaningful reading in a very different context. For the indifferent reader, actions do indeed speak louder than words, but the two can be linked very effectively.

Let us begin with a consideration of a rhythmic sound activity.

Reading and Rhythm

Sooner or later, no matter what scheme or system is followed, we have to face the problem of Phonics. Once the initial stage of acquiring a basic look-and-say vocabulary is passed, phonics become increasingly important as an essential component of the child's reading skill. It is by phonic and syllabic attack that unknown words are first solved, and progression from the domains of Look-and-Say achieved.

Now, although the alphabet has little value in its own right, it is a form of introduction to the components of words. It is not unusual for the backward reader to be unsure of his alphabet, let alone the sounds, with accompanying feelings of inferiority. Under these circumstances he tends to dread work with a straightforward alphabet card, and this in itself inhibits his efforts.

With such cases, a kinaesthetic approach has proved to be of material assistance. Appeal to the memory by this means is often employed when words or sentences are being memorised (*vide* Fernald and Keller) but that physical movement can be purposefully related to phonics is not widely realised.

The degree of difficulty present in learning phonims (or single sounds) is greater where the basic alphabet is not known, the child having to learn shape, name and sound formation together. Added to this is the order of the alphabet which, a law unto itself, has no obvious *raison d'être*.

The oral movement involved in making a given sound is small, and in the kinaesthetic approach a relatively large and rhythmical series of movements is added by the hands. Why

Two Visual-Verbal basic cards, showing the simultaneous presentation of word and picture.

An example of 'mirror writing' by a seven-year-old child of average intelligence.

this apparently extra imposition on the mind aids speech and reading processes is difficult to explain and well outside our practical terms of reference. Let us therefore carry straight on with details of the method, which could be called Sound Drill.

SOUND DRILL CHART			
1 Take your letter	2 Hold it up	3 Throw it away	4 Wait
Like this	Like this	Like this	Like this
A	says	a	—
B	says	b	—
C	says	c	and
D	says	d	— —
E	says	e	—

FIG. 13. The Sound Drill wall chart.

Each child holds at arm's length an imaginary box containing the alphabet and with his dominant hand selects a letter at a time, holding it up and discarding it in three rhythmical movements. Simultaneously he names and sounds the letter, following a wall chart constructed for this purpose. Movement, rhythm and speech are co-ordinated as follows:

Rhythm :	1	2	3	4
Movement:	Select	Exhibit	Discard	Pause
Speech :	A	says	'a'	—
	B	says	'b'	—
	C	says	'c'	and[1]
	D	says	'd'	—[2]
	E	says	'e'	— etc.

[1] Stress.   [2] Longer pause.

F

The wall chart, of course, consists of the speech section of the above only (Fig. 13). A column of words, taken as far as possible from known material and showing the sound in action, may be added:

P   says   'p'   (as in *pip*)

—but this should not be allowed to interfere with the basic rhythm, and should be used only for reference during the orthodox consolidation which will follow; that is, initial phonic analysis of words in work-books, games and reading books being used.

When children are ready to begin work with digraphs (or double sounds), the kinaesthetic approach may again be employed on the lines already indicated, using a similar chart. Finally, four essentials for success:

(*a*) Insist on the movements being large.

(*b*) Never call the wall chart 'the alphabet'.

(*c*) Perform the exercise right the way through with the group until the children are making the correct sound for every letter or digraph.

(*d*) Make the drill a short but regular part of every reading lesson.

Now this is an account of a technique that harnesses the power of movement and rhythm to help in the assimilation of sounds. But even broader approaches can be made.

Consider for a moment the plight of what we may term the 'Stagnant Readers'—children who have started their Junior School life with at least the beginnings of reading skill, yet who have made little or no subsequent progress. These are the children who seem stuck in the mud of reading; they find the effort of making the transition to new material very difficult, and they seem all too ready to accept defeat. Some even revert to being non-readers after a period of continuous failure.

There will be numerous reasons for this. There is always the possibility that they have made too early a start anyway and, as always, this has caused undue difficulty which in turn inhibits further progress. There are the shortcomings in speech, sight and hearing that we will look for as a matter of course. Too much laborious phonic drill may be at the bottom of lack of progress—and in other cases not enough! A balance needs to be maintained between strengthening the interest factor through word-whole methods and giving children the power of unlocking the meaning of new words through phonic approaches. That is why a 'sound-drill' even of the kinaesthetic variety needs to be brief.

Where the ordinary causes of reading backwardness do not seem to apply, the Stagnant Reader—Reluctant Reader is perhaps a happier phrase—may well be standing still for the simple reason that he has just lost interest. Our problem has become one of motivation—finding a way of showing him that reading *is* a skill worth having, and yet doing this outside the situation of the class reading lesson.

Reading games spring to mind as the obvious answer, but helping children with reading difficulties is an individual matter, and there will be children who will reject even this approach. 'Games,' they may think, 'games are what you play in the playground, not these silly old things you make in class.' And so, whilst they will suffer our efforts to help them, their general attitude may remain one of passive rejection. You can lead a horse to the water but you can't make it drink. Motivation must precede co-operation.

Live Reading

Bearing this in mind, it may pay us to attack from an entirely new angle the problem of children who are making no reading headway, using the few common words that they already know in conjunction with a series of *live* words presented against a *live* background.

There is no more effective way of bringing words to life than adding movement! The potential of correlating reading with P.E. is not widely realised, yet the advantages accruing from such a union are obvious. P.E. is a happy activity which provides a good medium for remedial work. It is a lesson in which the illiterate may outshine the scholar, and it is one of the few subjects during which it is possible to utilise rather than suppress the child's instinctive desire to learn through movement. From a psychological aspect, it is ideal.

This form of live reading can begin in the craft lesson when the class make sets of blank cards roughly 8″ by 4″. Alternatively they can collect the sheets of card of this size which separate layers in some cereal packets. Each child suggests a word, which is written in his book by the teacher. He is then given a set of plastic letters to use as templates (borrowed from the Infant department) and told to reproduce his word on his card, filling in with wax crayon. Meanwhile, the more advanced children proceed to make 'link' cards in the same way; for example:

I have a . . . This is my . . . Look at our . . . This great big . . . Children are allowed to see how their friends are getting on, and will learn many of each other's words in this way. During the last five minutes of P.E., the children wear their cards by means of attached string armholes. (See Fig. 14.)

FIG. 14. A card with string armholes attached. Other words which could be used are:

PLAY	IN	CAN	BUT	TALL	WALK
RUNS	OUT	RAN	YOU	CALL	TALK
WICKET	CRICKET	AND	HALL	WALL	CHALK
FIELD	I	JUMP	FALL	ALL	

Spinning the Platter forms a good starting-point and can be followed up with Crystal Palace, words being called out in place of names. Release can be played, the captured 'words' being formed into a sentence, completion of which constitutes outright victory. Sentence formation also provides a new form of Chain He, the chain chasing specific words which will fit on the end.

Team games are very popular. Teams of words can be haphazard, connected by some common theme, a sentence or, later on, phonic families. In these ways we can link kinaesthetic help to Word-Whole, Sentence and Phonic methods of learning to read.

Reading races are run, the first child in each team running to the back, reading every word as he does so. Frantic prompts should be ignored; child teaches child very quickly. Teams can sort themselves into alphabetical sequences or swop words to produce new sentences. Individual ball bouncing, spelling the word to the rhythm, is useful, the word being changed after an unbroken 'bounce through'.

A change from the children wearing cards is the carrying out of a completely silent P.E. lesson using large card operative words: *Begin, Stop, Four Teams, Free Running*, etc. This promotes quick word recognition.

Half a dozen cards per child gives a working vocabulary of roughly 200 words, enough in itself to give new life to reading. The real value of the scheme, of course, lies in changing the child's attitude to print before it becomes chronic.

Dramatic Reading

A third method connected with the kinaesthetic approach is also concerned with movement in the classroom, this time through the equally acceptable situation of the Drama lesson.

Dramatic activities are particularly pertinent at this stage of our consideration of help with reading, because of a danger inherent in any book preoccupied with method. The point that we need to bear in mind is that the remedial material and the skill with which it is used are generally applied to the end of assisting the child with his reading through his reading, *rather than through himself*. While this is of little significance when dealing with the child of average ability, it should be remembered that academic retardation is frequently accompanied by emotional difficulties, and often complicated by maladjustment that may be either the cause or the effect of the actual retardation. Where this is suspected as a root cause of reading deficiency, there is obviously a need for remedial work of a type that will help the child at the subconscious as well as the conscious level.

The value of dramatic work as a vital stage in child development is already widely recognised. Through its medium children can experiment with their emotions, indulge in self-projection and in general blow off emotional steam. Used with maladjusted children, it can effectively help to release inhibitions and resolve complexes.

We may agree that drama as a vehicle for remedial reading has the following desirable qualities, apart from its kinaesthetic potential:

(*a*) It is a great confidence builder.

(*b*) It arouses interest.

(*c*) It provides a reason for reading.

(*d*) It shows the relationship between sense and sentence in the tangible form of acting.

(*e*) It permits movement while learning, as opposed to prohibiting it. Movement relieves tension.

(*f*) It promotes *rapport* in that it is fun and not drudgery.

Two separate schemes are suggested below, the first for children of low I.Q. and the second for those whose failure cannot be attributed primarily to this cause. Both aim at success through success, as well as through the playing out of emotional disturbance.

1. At first movement is divorced from print. For a few lessons nothing but group mime and improvisation are attempted, the children being encouraged to express themselves with complete freedom. The idea of dramatising events suggested or experienced by children, or drawn from familiar stories is then put forward. One is selected, discussed and 'translated' by the teacher from the spoken word into a simplified and preferably repetitive play form, involving of course the written word.

From the master script we invite those who intend to act in the play to make individual copies, an activity which gives additional kinaesthetic reinforcement to the learning of the word shapes as well as opportunities for mutual aid through the pooling of word knowledge. As an ostensible check the play is now read back to the children, who follow their own copies. Then they go away to rehearse the words only in a corner. No direct help is given, but it is as well to include in each group a child who is sufficiently advanced to 'prompt' where necessary. Since each actor is also part author, it follows that he or she will have a fair idea of what the sentences signify. Incentive is heightened by the fact that, often for the first time, the fantasy-starved non-reader, cut off from the world of make-believe within the covers of books, is able to bring to life the little black symbols in front of him.

When a play can be read satisfactorily, it is learnt; often the two stages coincide. Some children will want to take scripts home to learn, and this generally indicates someone in the family who is willing to help. Provided that such help is given via the script, it is obviously beneficial, but should never be referred to in school.

The group now perform their play. Improvised costume

and make-up should be allowed because, although the performance is merely a means to an end, to the children it
represents an end in itself. We must seem to take the reading
involved for granted.

Three or four groups can operate at once in a class. When
a play has been performed, it is 'swapped' with another
group, who have gained sufficient knowledge of it from the
performance to enable them to make a start with reading and
performing. Scripts, however, are not exchanged. Every
child makes his own copy of each play in which he takes
part. These copies form the mechanical basis of his recovery;
they are in effect personal reading books but are never
treated as such. No teaching of reading is being undertaken,
only the acting of plays, and perhaps teaching of how to say
lines. The essence of the approach is its indirectness;
prompting, for instance, is allowed but telling a child a word
is not. We have a function as producers, but not as teachers
of reading.

Half a dozen plays of this nature will often serve to provide
the change of attitude, and the basic word knowledge necessary before work with books as such is resumed. When this
does take place it is a good plan to make a play from a
suitable part of each reading book as it is finished. Apart
from anything else, this is an interesting means of carrying
out repetitive revision.

2. The relatively bright child who can do almost anything
except read is generally acutely conscious of his shortcomings, especially if his classmates are not similarly handicapped. Such a child may not lack the innate ability to read,
but is prevented from doing so by conditions which he does
not understand, and over which he has little control—
Dyslexia, for example.

In order to short-circuit feelings of inferiority, the initial
dramatic material chosen must appear to be of a standard

compatible with the class's ability, and yet must make provision for remedial reading. An interesting point here is that, while the retarded reader of low I.Q. will eventually have to be exercised in the mechanical skills of reading that we have discussed previously, his counterpart of higher intelligence will generally absorb these as and when he really begins to read.

Some history and geography text-books conclude each chapter with a revision playlet. This consists of sufficient dialogue, usually six or seven lines, to prime an improvisation based on some aspect of the matter under consideration. Here is the right proportion of print to action contained in routine classwork, and therefore not associated with the experience of failure. In short, here is one ideal starting-point for the intelligent backward reader.

Several groups of children are allowed to improvise the scheme. The one containing the backward reader is never the first, and so this child has time to memorise a line or two that has to be read before his turn comes. Thus he becomes convinced of his ability to take part in an advanced verbal activity lasting perhaps ten minutes without difficulty.

Complete scenes from school plays may follow. At first the backward reader is given the shortest part, but this is heavily disguised by stressing the action. As his reading improves, the length of his part is gradually increased, but the weight of the part will not matter particularly to him. What will matter is that he is at one with the rest of the class in an aspect of reading, and is able to revel in gregarious normality. Handwriting and general English lessons based on the play of the moment will provide further kinaesthetic backing.

Once such a child realises his ability to take part in normal work of this kind the necessary emotional change may be brought about, and in a few months he may be reading as well as the boy in the next desk. The explanation is that, while his motions are absorbed and his conscious thought concentrated on the acting, he is able to make an indirect and uninhibited contact with print; the phobias and emotional 'blocs' associated with reading do not operate because the primary occupation (as far as he is concerned) is not reading, and for the same reason he is prevented from 'trying too hard'.

Between the two extremes mentioned there are numerous variations in ability, including the generally larger group of mediocre readers. Dramatic work, even if undertaken purely from a dramatic point of view, will benefit every one of these —and the 'forward' readers as well. Even for Dyslexic children, drama makes a refreshing and beneficial change from 'static' work.

Whilst kinaesthetic approaches (other than the direct help provided by writing and tracing) will not be so widely employed as more conventional methods, they are particularly valuable in 'difficult' cases, or where things are just not going according to plan.

Perhaps, on second thoughts, this may mean that we shall be using these techniques more often than we had planned!

Chapter 7

A 'Comic' Approach to Practical Reading

"The vocabulary of comics is very closely related to the child's state of articulation and language development. Thus those responsible for the production of comics, hard-headed businessmen for the most part, with no other end in view than profit, are achieving by one of the most popular playways what educationalists are striving to accomplish by the more stereotyped means of Infant Readers."— Scottish Council for Educational Research: *Studies in Reading*, Vol. 2

It would be a pity if in view of the stress that has been placed on the advantages of V-V material, and the snags implicit in the use of Look-and-Say, we underestimated the true worth of pictures in their own right, or indeed of the more conventional Word-Whole methods in general.

Children first come to associate enjoyment and meaning with those flat and comparatively small surfaces called book pages through pictures. Looked at in this light, picture books form the most natural beginning to the complex process of learning to read. Not only does the young child 'read' the meaning of the picture, or the series of pictures, but he is preparing himself for the process of learning to unlock the meaning contained in the smaller, squiggly 'pictures' of print.

There are, for instance, the basic physical skills involved in handling a book and manipulating pages. At a higher level, children become accustomed to the conventional yet arbitrary left-to-right sequence of meaning that leads to the establishment of correct eye movement. There is the assimilation and interpretation of various small details that give particular meaning to pictures, and this calls for the ability to focus the eyes on specific points a short distance away, which in turn demands concentration.

Apart from these considerations, children looking at pictures want to talk about them, and in this way pictures help in the development of verbal self-expression, and in the building up of word concepts, so that when these words are encountered later on in the form of print, children do at least know what they mean.

Perhaps, from our particular point of view, enjoyment is the most important part of looking at pictures. Enjoyment is the one thing that non-readers have learnt from bitter experience to exclude from contact with the printed page. Yet they can still enjoy 'just looking at the pictures', and so we have one tenuous attachment to pleasure through pages— provided that we are willing to accept and make use of the kind of material that children still regard as fun in its own right.

The Infant Primer is full of attractive pictures, but attractive only to the age range of children for whom they are specifically produced. We have already seen that using this type of book serves only to underline lack of ability and to accentuate feelings of inferiority. The content of the pictures will, in any case, have little or no appeal to the over-eights with whom we are concerned, and who will (quite rightly) see the activities depicted as babyish.

The happily increasing number of beautifully illustrated 'readers' for these somewhat older children (Ladybirds; Golden Pleasure Books, etc.) will be at once a source of pleasure and frustration, since the level of reading skill demanded is generally far too high to hold out much hope of progress to these already greatly discouraged cases of chronic failure. Again they are tacit reminders to the non-reader of his backwardness.

It is hardly surprising, therefore, that the only reading material that really attracts such children is the 'cheap, vulgar, nasty, trashy' comic. But how far are we justified in using such adjectives? And if children do like comics, would we not be better advised to make use of their interest in this direction to our ends of trying to teach them to read, rather than to pursue the more negative course of forbidding comics in the classroom and thus effectively pushing pleasure and reading even further apart?

Surely we have to admit that some of the modern comics are well produced, well illustrated and psychologically sound in content and outlook; periodicals like *Robin*, *Eagle* (*Boys' World*), *The Jolly Roger* and *Girl*. And, even if the pictures and stories in some of the other comics are aesthetically poor, they are at least, as our quotation at the head of this chapter points out, of intense interest to children. As far as we are concerned, there will be plenty of time to develop aesthetic standards once we have helped these less able children to acquire a minimal standard of reading skill. If, in order to achieve this, we begin with something linked to their interest that may be just impossible science-fiction or blood-and-thunder or pupils-getting-the-better-of-the-teacher, does it really matter? These situations are common enough in 'classical' literature: *Twenty Thousand Leagues Under the Sea*, *Treasure Island* or *Tom Brown's Schooldays*, for example. Some of the Greek legends, and even traditional nursery rhymes and fairy stories will be found guilty on the same counts if we insist on wearing literary blinkers. Each, surely, represents a stage of perfectly normal development through which all of us have passed. We should in fact be sorry for the person who asserts that he or she certainly never enjoyed 'trashy comics' as a child.

Let us consider, then, how the humble comic can help children over the first hurdle of acquiring a sight vocabulary of 50 to 60 words that will re-establish his confidence in his ability to deal with words, and give him a foothold on the following stage of dealing with books proper.

If children are encouraged to bring their old comics to school, a 'store' of material will soon be built up. The non-reader will be able to spend odd moments profitably by browsing through these comics which, as we have seen, is valuable pre-reading experience particularly suited to his needs and age. He may also enjoy the prestige of handling and 'reading' the magazines and periodicals that his more advanced friends enjoy, and which his parents perhaps might not buy him because they feel it would be a waste of money since he 'can't even read books for Infants'.

It is surprising how many of these children will soon be able to pick out the titles of the various comics, and the names of the main characters, particularly if they are allowed to take the comics into a corner with one or two other children, and talk (quietly!) about what intrigues them. Little of the vital action is lost through the inability to read and these central characters are mentioned over and over again, so that there are plenty of opportunities for picking out and consolidating names as they become known. It is from this tiny island of reading knowledge that our 'Comic Methods' stem, although again the emotional climate of enjoyment, interest, purpose and confidence contributes to their success. The inhibiting suspicion that sometimes attaches to 'special' (remedial) books and thinly disguised apparatus with its common denominator of backwardness in reading is circumvented. Children are psychologically freer to go forward.

However, let us keep away from this shadowy word 'psychology' and come closer to the theme of our book. As practising teachers we are more concerned with doing than eulogising or theorising. We begin by giving our non-reader an ordinary exercise book, and it is in fact possible to begin with an old, filled book that is no longer wanted, since in these first stages there will be no writing but only cutting out and sticking in. Or a special 'File' (see Chapter 9) may be constructed, but on the whole the exercise book is much simpler as a starting point.

On each page, up in the top right hand corner, the child prints a letter. He may do this in a variety of ways using crayons, paints, a felt pen, a stencil or a potato cut. He may prefer to cut a series of steps out of the right hand side of the book and print a letter on each step so as to produce an index system. But (traditional die-hards sit tight!) the letters which the child prints are in any order *but* alphabetical, this idea really belongs to a much later and more sophisticated stage.

The reason for this apparent travesty of teaching is two-fold: firstly, a straightforward alphabet savours of the Infant school work which we are trying so hard to avoid and, secondly, knowing the alphabet parrot fashion has no relation at all to reading; it has value only in that it provides a means of using classified material, indexes, etc., worthwhile activities certainly, but well outside our present terms of reference.

'Think of a letter,' the child is told. 'Print/stencil/draw/copy/trace/paint/crayon it up here on your first page. Or if you like, find that letter in a comic, cut it out and stick it in place. Now, when you have done that, try to find a word that you know, or two words that you know, beginning with the same letter, and stick them on the middle of the page. You must know what the words are before you can stick them in. And then do the same with the next page. Start a collection of words!'

Many comic titles and character captions are strongly

alliterative. This quality stresses the sound value of the initial letter, which is the least likely to be irregular, and is of course the most helpful, used in conjunction with the context, in trying to decide what a particular word may be. *I have a* . . . below a picture of a boat invites guesses of anything ranging from ship to yacht, and whilst the superstructure, sails, etc., provide a little guidance, the 'ber' or 'yer' is a more positive clue.

The sort of result that will be produced is D: Dan Dare, F: Freddy the Fearless Fly, K: Keyhole Kate, and so on. If captions deliberately misspell words as in Korky the Cat we can print the correct spelling on a piece of paper to be glued underneath, but leave the original untouched. It shows, in an unconventional way, that both 'C' and 'K' can have the same phonic value.

As the collection progresses, the child will find that some letters are not so easy to provide with a word. When this stage is reached we can give a little help by suggesting compromises like X: Exmouth on the Exe. Z: Zebra in the Zoo. The collection is completed by cutting out and sticking in place suitable pictures from the comics, or by a personal painting or drawing. The satisfaction of 'making a set'—of collecting—is a strong one, and the child will need little encouragement to make up a second book of a similar nature.

Although these two collections will consist of 'comic' words in the main, the children will have looked at many others in the process of searching for a suitable one, and repeated the sound of the initial letter over and over again in trying to match a word or phrase to a letter. Without being aware of what is happening, they will have acquired within their basic sight vocabulary a surprisingly high proportion of words that will occur, and that they will therefore be able to recognise, in 'ordinary' sentences and books. In the examples given, for example, the captions will break down to give *the, fear, ear, less, fly, key, hole, ate, an, dare, are, or* and,

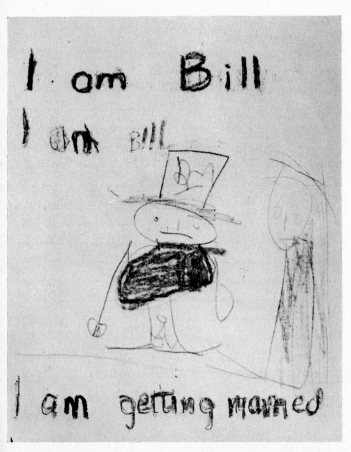

I am Bill

I am Bill

I am getting married

The first page in the Personal Work Book of a disturbed and backward child.

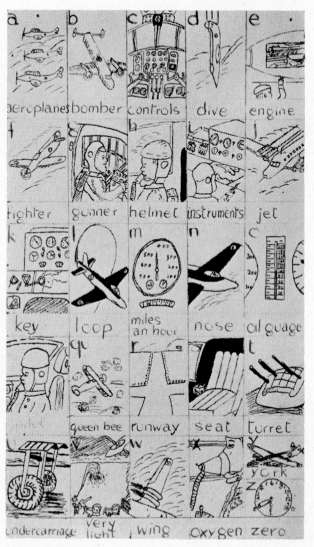

A phonic word chart made by a word-blind boy of 11 (reading age 6·4) who had a passion for aeroplanes.

in corrected form, *cork*. The next step, then, is to invite the backward reader to extend his new skill by making words from words. Without resorting to any new comic material he will suddenly find that he can conjure up another two or three sets of words which, with the aid of his knowledge of initial sounds, he will soon be able to read at sight.

All kinds of variations will readily suggest themselves from now on; we can even think in terms of sorting known words into alphabetical sequence. But the main thing is that we have actually got the non-reader to the point where he has material and 'books' that he can read—and we have done this, as it were, whilst he was looking the other way—concentrating on the comic. Children can look through each other's collections, learning to recognise a few additional words, or the ones in their own collections in a different context and setting. They can compete to see who gets the most words beginning with a given letter. They can swop individual words to complete collections, and they can make charts as described in Chapter 11.

One form of follow-up work that is particularly valuable is the construction of lists of common phrases from words cut out of comics and stuck together in a line. Each phrase or sentence is completed by finding a suitable word, cutting it out and sticking it into position at the end of the line, or at the beginning, in the case of the two lower specimen lists shown in Fig. 15.

Writing known material in a Personal Work Book will prove a satisfactory step back towards the general line of method we are following through this book, and the ultimate changeover from comic characters to 'normal' books is not as difficult as it might appear to be. Ultimately, children who have started to learn to read on comics will want to be able to read the sort of books that are used in the rest of the class or school, if only to show the world (and the cocky child in the desk opposite) that they are as capable of so doing as

FIG. 15. Lists of common phrases, which can be completed by words cut from comics and pasted in position.

anyone else. Then, in some of the better comics, well-known and well-loved near-classical stories are often presented in simplified strip form. Whilst the magnificence of language and the characteristics of style may be partially lost, the process of familiarisation with the story and the people in it does take place, and there is every chance that the child will want to read a fuller version of any story that has appealed to him in this form—once he possesses the skill in reading which will enable him to do so.

Like the stereotyped comic strip of the worst type, the use of the watered-down picture classic is a means to an end, a step in the right direction, and as such we may find an application here of the dictum: 'If you can't beat 'em, join 'em!'

Finally, for those of us who would prefer to 'vet' the material used in this way in the classroom, here is a 'comic approach' in which we can decide on the pictures used, and indeed on the words employed in conjunction with the pictures as well.

We select fifteen or twenty reasonably large pictures from comics or magazines of which we approve, and include blocks of two or three illustrations wherever possible. All the pictures are mounted on strips of white card in such a way that a space deep enough for two lines of writing is left underneath.

On the top line we print in bold capitals one single word describing or strongly connected with the picture, and on the second line a very short sentence, in script, about what is taking place. Thus we might begin with:

SPACE-SHIP
The space-ship takes off.

or in a series of three, as in Fig. 16.

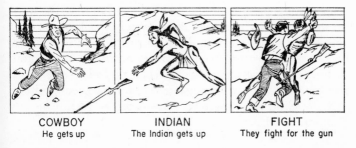

COWBOY
He gets up

INDIAN
The Indian gets up

FIGHT
They fight for the gun

FIG. 16.

The choice of words used will to some extent be determined by the theme of the pictures, but it should still be possible, because of the overlap of meaning, to incorporate a fair degree of repetition, involving the use of the commoner words that occur in most remedial reading schemes.

The series of pictures is pinned in correct sequence round the walls of the classroom. We should do this one morning well before any member of the class arrives, and we should deliberately avoid mentioning that fact that it has been put up, or any reference to its purpose. If children do ask direct questions about it we can indicate vaguely that it is a story around which at some time we might possibly be doing some English work. And of course such a sequence of pictures *can* be used as a starting point for creative writing. Let us confine our attention for the moment, however, to the effect on the non-readers in the class.

These children, goaded by curiosity, will eventually be driven to ask their classmates (or even their teacher!) what the writing beneath says. Or they may guess. Because their concentration and interest have been intensified through sheer curiosity, they will tend to remember what certain words and phrases are, and this knowledge will help them to learn and recall the meaning of the rest of the 'strip'.

Once a child is able to recognise and recall the main word underneath a picture, he should be allowed to trace the word on to the appropriate page in an exercise book or file kept specially for this purpose. If he can read the word ARROW on the tenth picture, then he traces ARROW at the bottom of the tenth page in his book. When the relative sentence has been mastered, this is also traced in the correct position, and the child adds his own version of the picture in any medium he wishes.

As with the previous 'comic' techniques, there is a strong appeal to the child's natural desire to collect things. In this case, it is the complete story. As one by one the gaps in the growing book disappear, excitement mounts and at the point of completion there is a feeling of pride and achievement.

The next phase consists of selecting a series of pictures that will make a complete story and mounting these on individual cards in much the same way as before except for the fact that there are two short sentences underneath, in place of the single word and sentence. These sentences will demand a little thought from us in that they must be short and repetitive, yet they must cover adequately the action involved in the story. Sometimes a complete page in a comic will provide us with the basic set of pictures, and where this is the case repetition should prove to be less of a problem. The cards are pinned around the classroom—though by no means in the correct sequence.

This set of pictures is used in much the same way, children tracing or copying the sentences as they find out what each says, but there is the additional complication (which adds to the fun) of trying to decide which picture should come where in the book. For this reason it is better to use a File, so that completed sheets can be shifted around experimentally, and this of course means that sentences are read over and over again as children try to relate them to the pattern of the story. This is also a very good means of stressing comprehension—that 'reading' means 'reading for meaning' right from the start.

An added complication is to make and mix up two sets of comic story cards and let children sort out which is which as they come to know the sentences. This really does involve a great deal of rereading, and in an interesting and purposeful setting.

The final stage of this method is to use a double sheet of comic material on which every other 'frame' is obliterated by blanks of paper on which are written sentences that bridge the gap in the meaning. This will reinforce the fact that print does add something to a story; 'bubbles' of talk over characters' heads will also help to do this.

Whichever paths we choose to follow from this point onwards, as regards techniques, it is surely no bad thing to keep up the pile of comics; preferably good comics, but at all events material that children may read 'just for fun'.

Because, to their way of thinking, this is one of the most important reasons for bothering to learn to read anyway.

Chapter 8

Material Matters

"At every stage at the right time, children need methodical help."—
H.M.S.O.: *Primary Education*

By now, the central theme of this book will have become
abundantly clear: that success in practical reading hinges on
changing the child's attitude towards this skill that so far has
baffled and rebuffed him.

The methods by which we try to bring about this change,
the techniques and approaches that are designed to rebuild
the capital of confidence that continual failure has destroyed,
are really no more than variations on our central theme. If the
techniques are looked on as flavouring, the basic ingredients
—enjoyment, purpose, meaning and, above all, immediate
success—should still be there for the child to taste.

We have looked at some of the ways in which these basic
ingredients can be incorporated into remedial approaches,
and we have tried to show the value of playing games
initially, as opposed to 'remedial reading sessions' or just
plain 'reading lessons', but for the busy class teacher the
setting up of a stock of bits and pieces can present other
problems.

Such people, it is hoped, will start off by agreeing with us
that the use of apparatus and games has earned a very

definite place in remedial reading, especially during the initial stages characterised by lack of confidence, interest and basic word knowledge. The value of this material, is, however, often weighed and found wanting in terms of time and money expenditure, both of which are economically rather than directly related to reading, but which nevertheless have to be recognised as factors of some account. There is, fortunately, a practical answer to this problem which if not a complete solution in itself comes very near to being so, and which merits special consideration towards the end of winter.

The indoor toys and games which children are given as Christmas and birthday presents sometimes last for days, sometimes for years, but seldom for ever. Consisting for the most part of cardboard or wood, they gradually get broken or are rendered useless by the loss of bits and pieces. In this state they remain around the house until the spring-cleaning, when they are quietly placed in the rubbish bin. Now, if we make an appeal at this time for broken or unwanted games, it may well result in a motley assortment of odds and ends which can quickly, cheaply and profitably be transformed by the retarded readers themselves into reading aids for their own use.

The word 'profitably' is used in its widest sense, since one of the headaches of the class teachers we have in mind is this question of what children who are unable to read can be doing whilst other more able groups are occupied with activities that demand either reading skill or the teacher's personal supervision and help.

In the cutting, measuring, sticking and general putting together of apparatus, there is scope for developing skills and attitudes which, although perhaps not directly connected with reading, are nevertheless part and parcel of those essential background ingredients we have mentioned. There is the sense of purpose and the feeling of doing something worth while that forms part of a practical contribution to group work. There is the feeling of achievement in the successful completion of the task, which adds to the child's self-respect. There is the concentration and deliberation involved, the social skills of sharing, waiting and co-operating, and the infinitely valuable opportunity of earning praise and approval—of being accepted as a worth-while person. And, of course, when the stage of making the parts concerned with words is reached, the tracing, copying, lettering, etc., afford opportunities for becoming familiar with the words as they are produced, in a relaxed atmosphere, free from the inhibiting tension and undesirable undertones that frequently form an effective bloc to reading progress in more conventional settings.

To come back to the mass of miscellaneous material that we have suggested will turn up in our classrooms, it is important to ensure that the children obtain permission from their parents before bringing things, otherwise Johnny Nonreader may turn up with the beautiful 3-D book given to his little brother last week, which is not really playing the game.

The next practical point we have to consider is how to fit our apparatus-making sessions into the school day. Ideally, we would have such small groups of children in our classes that this one would solve itself, but ours is a practical book, and we have to face the unpalatable fact that classes are large; far, far too large for effective teaching in small groups, let alone individuals (what would be a fair ration of individual attention per child during a 40-minute lesson with an unstreamed class of, say, 47 children?).

However, there are quite a few lessons during which our special group can get on with their 'project on games': handwork, of course, or optional periods; during art or craft; as part of the English work or during particular reading periods. And, once children discover the infinite possibilities of adapting bits and pieces to create new games, once they begin to taste the thrill of bringing their ideas to life, this becomes the sort of out-of-school activity that can usefully be linked with the Reading Club described in Chapter 11.

It is far better to encourage the children to experiment with what is available than to copy slavishly the ideas that we may put forward to start them off. Certain basic techniques and adaptations will be necessary. The simplest and most direct apparatus, apart from V-V material, is that made from old packs of cards and card games. Throw away any that are badly torn and clean the remainder thoroughly with bread crumbs. Cover the faces with blanks of white paper and trim the pack to a uniform size, either en masse with a guillotine, or as a class exercise in measuring, ruling and cutting to give dimensions, each child preparing three or four cards. Common words are then printed on the blanks, every card being duplicated. The words should be suggested by the children, or, better still, found by them on the objects that are clearly labelled and waiting to be discovered in the classroom or home: *chocolate*, *Monday*, *ink*, etc. We shall find that the children are anxious to take over the writing of the words once they see what is wanted. These packs are now ready to be used for a variety of word games: Snap, Pelmanism, alphabetical sorting and so on.

In the case of old packs which have damaged or defaced backs and so are unsuitable for use as above, the children should cover both sides with blank paper, printing a word on one side and drawing, tracing or sticking a picture that illustrates the word on the other. In this way sets of foolproof reading cards are built up, a child first attempting to read a word and then referring to the picture on the reverse side to see if he has read it correctly. This is a particularly useful series to employ as a means of 'word motivating' renovated race games, each player trying to read three words before moving, as follows:

    1 word right   ..   forward 1 square

2 (consecutive) words ..   forward 3 squares
3 words   ..   forward 6 squares and another
                                      turn

Some of the rules pertaining to these games in their
original form may have to be modified; it is inadvisable, for
instance, to insist on a '6' being scored before starting. The
number of cards in each pack should vary with the ability of
the child. For a non-reader, half a dozen words are enough;
these will be thoroughly known by the end of a game or
two, and hence by this means alone it is possible to build up a
basic sight vocabulary in a comparatively short time. As
with V-V, almost any form of race game can be adapted for
use with these cards.

The spinning or revolving arm type of game, after any
necessary mechanical repairs and perhaps some painting, can
be used to indicate which of a dozen small packs of cards
encircling it must be correctly read by the spinner in order
to score a point, or avoid elimination. Cards for this activity
can bear a simple sentence instead of a single word, preferably one which can be clearly and unmistakably represented
on the reverse.

If desired, each of the small packs can be a miniature story
based on the reading books which will be subsequently
employed.

Old sets of dominoes can be renovated and used in a
similar fashion. They are well suited to simple phonic work,
the player being required to put down a piece bearing a word
whose first letter is the same as the last of the end word.
Sound 'family' games, too, can be played.

Odd figures, animals and vehicles can be mended and
used either as counters in games or to represent dramatically
scenes from the books being read. Alternatively, they can
be glued to bases on which are written descriptive words
or short sentences. Children sometimes evolve the most

complicated games amongst themselves with this material, and this should be encouraged and made the subject of discussion and brief written work. Labelled football teams are particularly popular, and there is a great deal of scope in transfers and league activity; with older children, it is even possible to link such work with the sports page of the local paper.

The electrical 'question and answer' game, which is deservedly popular with children, can be a tremendous incentive to the backward in reading. If the class is fortunate enough to produce one of these, it is worth spending a little time on the contacts, wiring and body, although completely rebuilding it is sometimes more satisfactory because then the finished product can be made sufficiently strong to stand up to the strains of classroom life. For those who are not electrically minded, the principle of the wiring is illustrated in Fig. 17. The actual conversion to a reading game is very simple. A word and relevant picture are substituted for each question and correct answer. A more complicated use is to make the game a mechanical brain. A series of words or sentences, each bearing a number, are pinned on the wall. On another wall a corresponding series of pictures bearing letters are mounted. If a child decides that Card 3 says *aeroplane*, he finds the letter on the appropriate picture, perhaps M, and then plugs in 3 and M, which are so arranged as to produce a light.

What about word building?

Occasionally, even in this day and age of progressive toys, a child may bring along some sort of word-building material. It may be the remains of a set of plastic letters, it may be what is left of a Scrabble outfit (what a stimulus this game can prove to our more advanced readers), and it may even be word syllables harking back to the methods of the monitorial system!

Now less able children look constantly for any kind of

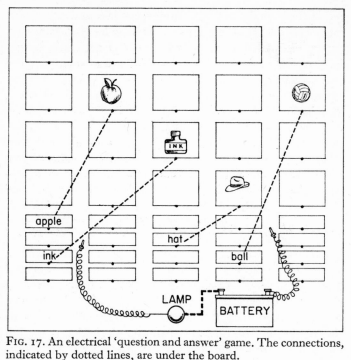

Fig. 17. An electrical 'question and answer' game. The connections, indicated by dotted lines, are under the board.

system in reading. Once they have a basic sight vocabulary they want to know 'the way' to read other words. Unfortunately, as we have seen, this is a question to which there is no wholly satisfactory answer when dealing with the English language. All we seem able to offer is the somewhat unpredictable system of sounding letters. But this, of course, is better than nothing. Building words is a way of drawing attention to specific letter sequences that are responsible for making any one word what it is (setting aside such ambiguities as *row*!).

Whilst word-building is not, therefore, to be viewed as a primary method of teaching children to read, it has, we may feel, been unfairly excluded from secondary and consolidating stages. If children suggest making lettered cubes (as described in Chapter 3), we should encourage them. If they want to make a simple Scrabble-type game of their own, can it do anything but good? If they wish to make straightforward alphabets and then cut them up and build words as many of us did as children, let us remember that there is more than one way of cooking a goose.

We may go further than this tacit acceptance, and actively support the construction of word-building material from blank postcards or pieces of card cut from the tops of old boxes. But we should give some thought to the question of the words used, bearing in mind that these older backward readers will no longer be interested in the *at*, *rat*, *rattle*, *prattle* type of material.

In the first place, it is desirable that the words we employ should be connected by meaning and related to a central theme or object. This should be within the cycle of the child's experience and strongly reinforced by interest. Phonic examples should be used within the limits imposed by context, and in any case patterns of similar shape but dissimilar sound avoided. Look at Card 1 in Fig. 18. A proportion of common words may be included in the first column so as to enable the child to attempt the whole of the card with the minimum of help from his teacher or group leader. It is worth noting that making these cards can form a useful exercise in English for more advanced children.

By cutting out a series of words on card strips of three standard sizes and drawing a visual representation of the final word on its reverse side, various 'puzzles' utilising this idea are easily made. A card frame will serve to keep completed strips in place, and the whole is self-corrective in that the picture illustrates the finished word, which must of course contain the preceding words. These in turn are graduated in length (Card 2, Fig. 18). When not in use, the

CARD 1   The Garden

or	for	fork
or	order	border
we	weed	weeds
see	seed	seedlings
an	man	manure
lot	lots	plots
ear	hear	shears
us	rush	brush
row	arrow	barrow
edge	hedge	hedging

OPTIONAL SPACE
FOR ILLUSTRATION

CARD 2   The Tool Box

am	ham	
an	pan	spanner
I	ice	vice
am	lamp	clamp
is	his	chisel
it	its	bits
it	spirit	spirit-level
crew	screw	screwdriver
and	sand	sandpaper
in	pin	pincers

Fig. 18.

words can either be kept in a labelled box or placed with the frame in a manila envelope.

A complete reversal of normal procedure may be found helpful in the early stages. The child refers to the picture in order to decipher the longest word, a process which often fixes it firmly in his mind by virtue of the extra interest and concentration invoked, and then finds the preceding words by matching and comparison. In the course of trial, error and elimination, the child is repeatedly called upon to sound letters as well as to recognise the smaller and more common words. This process is an excellent disguise for what amounts to quite dull repetitive drill. An additional advantage is that the solution of the *longer* words breeds confidence in ability to read the *shorter* ones, despite the fact that at this stage the level of difficulty is often inversely proportional to length because of the unfortunate and confusing pattern similarity found amongst the smaller basic words of our language.

Another idea for using this method is to stick a suitable picture on the back of a card. Numbers on the relative parts of the picture coincide with a set alongside the words on the front, thus providing the necessary clues and correction (Card 3, Fig. 19). Obviously many other variations are possible and, most important, the children are able to do a considerable amount of work on their own, a factor in remedial reading seldom given the consideration it merits.

Card 4 in Fig. 19 shows what can be made of proprietary names, in this case car makes. Interest dominates vocabulary, but for near non-readers a little 'jam' sometimes gives a surprising edge to their reading appetites. Sweet or cigarette cards (and it is extraordinary how many children will still produce them) may be used in conjunction with such lists.

Apart from the instances mentioned, we should not in this situation use too many pictures. Visual props should be supplemented by a fundamental desire to read brought about by interest and success. Series of cards should gradually

CARD 4   The Car Park

arm	arms	Armstrong
in	tin	Austin
Ben	bent	Bentley
or	for	Ford
ill	hill	Hillman
or	organ	Morgan
roll	rolls	Rolls-Royce
in	sing	Singer
be	beam	Sunbeam
and	stand	Standard

CARD 3   My Bicycle

1	poke	spoke	
2	eel	heel	wheel
3	am	lamp	headlamp
4	rake	brake	brake lever
5	or	for	fork	forks
6	in	ink	inks	links
7	in	ring	spring	springs
8	add	addle	saddle
			saddle-bag
9	a	an	ran	rank	crank
10	a	an	and	hand
			handle	handle-bars

CARD 3   My Bicycle

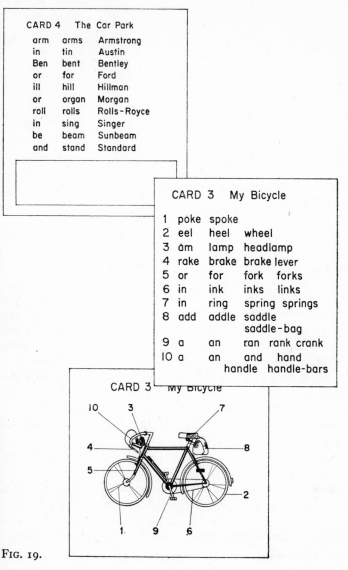

FIG. 19.

H

```
CARD  5    The  Kitchen

   in        ink       sink
   us        dust      duster
   and       hand      door-handle
   as        gas       gas-cooker
   ace       lace      fireplace
   all       wall      wall-paper
   able      table     table-cloth
   or        floor     floor-cloth
   so        soap      soap-dish
   owe       towel     roller-towel
```

FIG. 20.

increase in difficulty, and a step in this direction is shown in Fig. 20 where external words are introduced in compound or hyphenated form, the known half of the word leading the child to the whole, having regard to the central theme.

Each card example shown is designed to fill the back of a postcard. If we use a typewriter, double-spacing will leave room for an illustration if desired. A series of typed cards takes little time to produce and the result is both uniform and legible.

As soon as a child is able to read a given card, he should copy out the words in an exercise book set aside for this purpose; a drawing or two will be useful here. Opposite each set of words, a few simple questions demanding repetitive answers should be written in script for consolidation and comprehension, and we are then back to the 'Work Book' or 'File' stage.

As we have already tried to point out, the underlying advantages of all these approaches, although less obvious than the narrower technical ones, are in some ways of greater importance. Children feel that they are doing something useful, constructive and entertaining, yet concretely connected with the printed word. There is this sense of contributing and sharing, and a fostering of both *esprit de corps* and *rapport*. From the resultant sense of purpose and belonging can spring the beginnings of progress. This is remedial reading in its true sense.

Chapter 9

Reading by Numbers

"The success which children attain in learning to read is closely related to the satisfaction they find in their experience with reading."
—Ruth Strickland

Let us return again to one of the most difficult problems that confront us as class teachers: that posed by a single backward or retarded reader in a group of children whose reading standard generally is satisfactory.

We have already looked into ways of helping such children if they have specific disabilities like Dyslexia, and we have seen that dramatic activity is a situation in which the weak reader can make a new start without drawing undue attention to his shortcomings. This is, of course, particularly useful when the child in question has some liking for or ability in acting.

Whilst drama as a subject has much to recommend it for the sometimes emotionally starved backward reader, should his interests or strength lie in other directions we should try wherever possible to link his reading work to whatever it may be that absorbs him, or that he happens to be good at.

To give a fairly obvious example, a boy whose passion is football may well respond best to material he collects concerned with the game. He can cut out pictures of his favourite stars and teams, and label them. He can compile brief, simple coaching hints with the aid of his teacher. He can make lists of results, and keep a football diary of the school fixtures and friendly matches. His initial V-V material will consist of words like *boots*, *goal-keeper* and *ball* and, although the level of reading difficulty may seem high, the book which he is likely to be most willing to tackle will be one about the game he loves so much.

Motivation, the discovery of a reason to want to read, is so very important. The interests and individual abilities of children, therefore, concern us very much.

Where a child's strength lies in a subject like Geography, the line of approach—travel brochures, advertisements, posters, maps and so on—is again clear enough. His Work Book and File (see Chapter 10) will quickly fill with material that stimulates, intrigues and delights. For him, the process of relearning to read has purpose; he can at least see where he is going. He is not just 'learning to read' all over again, with the unpleasant memories and feelings that this process inevitably brings.

Rather less obvious is the line of approach we should employ in the case of a child who has some little skill in number operations, yet can hardly read at all. The question of what to do about this in the Arithmetic lesson arises constantly. What can the backward reader do when his classmates are busy with word-sums or problems? The situation is far from unknown in B and even A stream classes.

To exclude this type of sum entirely from his work is, of course, to pave the way for feelings of inferiority, but what else can be done? The answer may lie in the correlation of both subjects—or, really, in the correlation of all three R's. Few non-readers are unable to count up to double figures and, on this simple premise, it is possible to build a structure of arithmetical words and terms. At the same time, the basic and most important number concepts will be greatly strengthened.

Figures, even to the eye of the non-reader, present a bold and comparatively distinct pattern which can be translated without difficulty into the spoken word. Thus, $1+2=3$ becomes *One and two are* (or *make*) *three*. If the figures are used as a sort of shorthand clue, the reverse will hold true: *One and two are three.* The child looks at the accompanying 'clue': $1+2=3$, and is able to 'translate' the words.

We start off by making a list of number names from *one* to *ten*, each with its clue:

Name	*Clue*
one	1
two	2
three	3
etc.	

We go straight on to addition without labouring the initial stage, and a number of variations become possible; final choice is a matter for the individual teacher, bearing in mind the type of arithmetical phrase used in the school for the sake of later continuity. Here is one possibility:

Addition	*Clue*
One and nine are ten	$1+9=10$
Two and eight are ten	$2+8=10$
Three and seven are ten	$3+7=10$
etc.	

The table should be copied out on a sheet of paper and practised. After sufficient questioning, the clue columns should be cut off by each child and used only when in doubt or for checking.

Immediately, the child will be able to tackle word-sums with the rest of the class; different sums but nevertheless word-sums, which is the important thing to him:

Two boxes and five boxes are ? boxes.

Seven sweets and three sweets are ? sweets.

Subtraction logically comes next. We may find that the most likely mistake to make when carrying out the first part of this scheme is in moving too slowly instead of the more common one of forcing the pace. We must not allow interest to flag because one table is becoming stale. If necessary, we can write out a variation of the same step, but we should not be afraid to move on! The remarks prefacing the addition table apply again.

Subtraction	*Clue*
Ten take away one leaves nine	$10 - 1 = 9$
Ten take away two leaves eight	$10 - 2 = 8$
Ten take away three leaves seven	$10 - 3 = 7$
etc.	

Or we may prefer:

One from ten leaves nine	1 from $10 = 9$
Two from ten leaves eight	2 from $10 = 8$

As with addition, the clues should be cut off after a reasonable degree of proficiency has been attained. Nouns with which the child is already familiar or may suggest can be added, so that the table becomes a series of Look-and-Say sentences:

	Clue
Ten Red Indians	10 Red Indians
take away	
Three Red Indians	$- 3$ Red Indians
leaves (or equals)	
Seven Red Indians	$= 7$ Red Indians

For the more (arithmetically) advanced child, one might use:

One shilling take away one penny leaves elevenpence	$1s. - 1d. = 11d.$
Ten pints take away eight pints leaves two pints	$10 \text{ pt.} - 8 \text{ pt.} = 2 \text{ pt.}$
Two pints make one quart	$2 \text{ pt.} = 1 \text{ qt.}$

Or even:

Three-eighths from five-eighths $\frac{3}{8}$ from $\frac{5}{8} = \frac{2}{8}$
     leaves two-eighths
Two-eighths are one quarter $\frac{2}{8} = \frac{1}{4}$

At this stage the child should be able to recognise the names of low numbers, plus the relative instructions dealt with so far. This work may well be below the standard he has attained in purely mechanical sums, but the return of self-confidence at the price of a little time is a good bargain. Actually he will have advanced in that he is now able to deal with genuine word sums.

It is not necessary to deal with number names after ten individually. These will be learnt in the process of tackling the next type of table: combined multiplication and division. Doubtless the form of wording used here will not meet with universal approval, but it can easily be adapted to suit all requirements. It is probably most effective to know tables all ways, i.e.:

$$4 \times 11 = 44 \quad 4)44 = 11 \quad 11 \times 4 = 44 \quad 11)44 = 4$$

—but this is a complication where Johnny Nonreader is concerned. So:

One times two is two	$1 \times 2 = 2$
Two into two goes once	$2)2 = 1$
Two times two are four	$2 \times 2 = 4$
Two into four goes twice	$2)4 = 2$
Three times two are six	$3 \times 2 = 6$
Two into six goes three times	$2)6 = 3$
etc.	

Word sums on or involving this table follow, and children are allowed to keep a reference copy in the back of their books. This, needless to say, is a figureless version.

At this juncture it is a good plan to introduce the list of Key Number Words shown below. It is made up of words which recur constantly in problems, and a few words should be learned at a time; some can be incorporated in V-V material, but most will have to be learned the hard way.

KEY NUMBER WORDS

Add *s*, *ing*, *ed*, *ly*, *er* to form compounds, but teach as individual syllables, or 'couplings'.

Aa	*Bb*	*Cc*	*Dd*	*Ee*	*Ff*
add	between	carry	depth	each	fair
all	bill	cost	divide	earn	far
altogether	borrow	count	down	end	feet
area	both			equal	florin
away	bought			every	foot
				exact	for

Gg	*Hh*	*Ii*	*Jj*	*Kk*	*Ll*
gain	half	if	job	keep	left
gallon	half-crown	in		kept	length
game	heavy	inch			lent
gave	how	inside			lose
give	hundred-weight	is			lost
		it			lot

Mm	*Nn*	*Oo*	*Pp*	*Qq*	*Rr*
make	need	of	part	quality	receipt
many	new	old	pence	quantity	receive
money	note	open	penny	quart	reserve
more	number	out	piece	quarter	rest
much		ounce	pint	question	right
multiply		owe	pound		run
			price		

Ss	*Tt*	*Uu*	*Vv*	*Ww*	*Yy*
save	take	under	value	weight	yard
sell	times	unsold	various	what	you
share	ton	use		when	your
shilling	total			where	
sixpence	towards			which	
spend				whose	
sold				why	
some					
sum					
subtract					

From this point onwards, we may standardise our procedure. Each table is dealt with as detailed in the example and whatever mechanical work is set consists of part figures and part words. As it becomes increasingly necessary to learn the tables *thoroughly* before moving on, progress will now tend to slow up, but having got as far as this the child's desire for yet another table and his consciousness of progress will act as a spur to his efforts; the danger of staleness mentioned earlier on will recede.

The 12 times table may be called the Magic Table, because it enables the child to do many types of new sums quickly and easily. Sometimes it pays to deal with this table after, say, the 4 times, so that practical sums involving money and length can be worked satisfactorily without delay. More advanced exercises can be made from the normal linear, weight and wet measure tables, and if these lines are followed, it should not be long before the child's problem ability is not far short of his number skill. A point we should watch is not to set problems requiring a great deal of thought while the child is mastering the art of obtaining figures from words. If we make them as easy, arithmetically, as possible, a long line of ticks appears in Johnny Nonreader's book. Encouragement is a great thing.

One of the attractions of this scheme is that it can be entered upon at any stage without departing from the underlying principle. Any degree of difficulty is achieved by mere 'translation' and any number of stage exercises and variations come readily to hand.

THE MAGIC TABLE

One times twelve is twelve	$1 \times 12 = 12$
Twelve into twelve goes once	$12)12 = 1$
Twelve pence make one shilling	$12d. = 1s.$
Twelve inches are one foot	$12'' = 1'$
Two times twelve are twenty-four	$2 \times 12 = 24$
Twelve into twenty-four goes twice	$12)24 = 2$

etc.

Chapter 10

A Book for the Backward Reader

"It is necessary that these pupils, who for so long have failed, should not fail again by being faced at an early stage of progress with a too difficult book."—Duncan: *Backwardness in Reading*

The title of this chapter, particularly when read in conjunction with the quotation that follows it, is a little misleading. We must say straight away that there is no more any one book for the backward reader than there is any one method.

Remedial reading, as we have seen, starts and keeps well clear of books. But somewhere along the line contact will have to be re-established with the printed page. V-V cards, games, apparatus and the like form a happy little world away from the cares and challenges of real reading. Like the lotus eaters, the backward readers may be loath to leave this land of ease and pleasure, and so we must try to ensure that the journey back to reality is smooth and successful.

Given half a chance, failure will do more than rock the boat; it will wreck our efforts. With this in mind we are going to demand a number of things from the remedial reading schemes that we choose to follow up our initial work with these children. Even before the first book is opened we shall be looking for bright, attractive covers, preferably bearing the sort of title and picture that will make the reader anxious to know what happens in the story.

As to the story itself, this must appeal to the older child— but through the skilled use of a limited number of words. There must be bold print, short sentences and plenty of graphic illustrations that really do help in deciding what the words will be about.

Things to do, other than just reading, should be incorporated in chapter endings, but the whole should be short enough for the reader to finish fairly quickly, and there will need to be more books of similar standard and layout to give opportunities for the consolidation of the new word knowledge gained. It is an advantage if these books take the form of amusing comprehension tests, or even crossword puzzles, so that the child, in addition to reading for meaning right from the start, is given a moral boost. His own stock will also rise in proportion to the number of books he finds himself able to deal with as a result of these first encounters, and so the words he tackles should be common ones. Some provision for simple but interesting phonic work is useful, too.

Let us hasten to say that we are not demanding the impossible. Sufficient schemes to meet all our requirements are given in the books named on page 126. The one danger is that we may, after looking at a single scheme chosen at random, decide that it fits the bill and that is the end of the matter. One scheme may possibly be better than another in certain respects, or at a certain stage, but once we have introduced books, the more of them that are just lying around to be picked up and looked at the better. Different schemes will also mean that a child who has reached a certain point in reading skill will be able to read a wide variety of books and obtain the consolidation of skills that we discussed earlier on.

There are scores of attractive remedial schemes, plus hundreds of what might be called supplementary books of a non-remedial nature. The superbly illustrated Ladybird books alone will provide a choice of nearly 200 titles, and it is often a great advantage to have a book of this kind to give to the reluctant reader with a particular interest in some sport, hobby or sphere beyond the confines of remedial material.

A comprehensive survey of the books available is contained in the following:

A Survey of Books for Backward Readers (U.L.P., 1956)

A Second Survey of Books for Backward Readers, Univ. of Bristol Institute of Education (U.L.P., 1962)

Help in Reading, S. S. Segal, Chairman, the Guild of Teachers of Backward Children (National Book League, 1964).

To single out specific books for comment would be outside our present terms of reference, but nevertheless we would call attention to the Beginner Book, *Hop on Pop* (Seuss, Collins, 1964) for two reasons. Firstly, that it escapes mention in the publications listed above, and secondly it is eminently suitable for work with Dyslexic children, both from the point of view of the highly unorthodox content and presentation and, more important still, because it presents all new words initially in large capitals.

Notwithstanding all that we have said about the requirements for remedial reading schemes, the crucial point remains that at which the transfer from reading activities to reading proper takes place. We make no apology for underlining the fact that books will still, for the near non-readers, be linked to feelings of failure, frustration, inadequacy and hostility; symbols and reminders of those early, awful days when people may have kept up a constant tirade of, 'Come on! You know what that says, surely! You can do it if you try! Oh, do make an effort! Don't be so silly—of course it's not *This*; it's *Here*. Use your eyes!'

We earnestly hope that we are being unjust in giving this imaginary quotation. But where anything on these lines *has*

been said, can we wonder that the children concerned sub-
consciously resolve to shut books out of their lives for good
and all?

Our motto during this delicate stage of transfer should be,
'Softly, softly, catchee monkey.' Things must happen
gradually, and some piece of apparatus is needed, in the
words of the famous advertisement, to 'bridge that gap'. Books,
certainly, will be about in the classroom so that children can
at any stage, *if they wish*, browse through them, looking at the
pictures and even trying to read little bits here and there,
but the first stages of transfer are perhaps most happily and
effectively made through 'books' that retain something of the
spirit of the reading activities; books, in other words, that
the children make for themselves.

Since the earliest attempts at reading printed material may
be captions, advertisements, comics and product labels, the
first 'book' can be a loose-leaf folder in which the children
keep their collection. Children love loose-leaf files, and the
measuring, cutting and concentration involved in making
them is in itself good pre-reading training. Such a prized
personal possession brings with it a very positive emotional
attachment as compared with the negative and inhibiting
feelings which may persist in connection with 'ordinary'
books. In this way, therefore, a 'Personal File' has a contribution to make in its own right, apart from its contents, to
progress in reading.

The simplest form of file is made from an empty corn
flake packet. Once a few have been made, it is a good idea to
hang up a card of printed instructions in the classroom for the
benefit of other children who want to know how it is done
(and for the benefit, of course, of the less able readers who,
having made a file, are away to a head start in reading what
the card says). If the card carries simple diagrams as well, it
becomes Look-and-Say material, with a very definite purpose apart from just 'reading'. Fig. 21 shows such a card.

MAKE THIS FILE

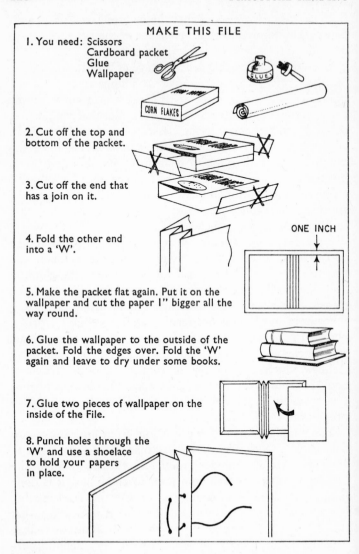

1. You need: Scissors
             Cardboard packet
             Glue
             Wallpaper

2. Cut off the top and bottom of the packet.

3. Cut off the end that has a join on it.

4. Fold the other end into a 'W'.

ONE INCH

5. Make the packet flat again. Put it on the wallpaper and cut the paper 1" bigger all the way round.

6. Glue the wallpaper to the outside of the packet. Fold the edges over. Fold the 'W' again and leave to dry under some books.

7. Glue two pieces of wallpaper on the inside of the File.

8. Punch holes through the 'W' and use a shoelace to hold your papers in place.

Fig. 21.

This is the simplest and most speedily built version. There are many possible variations and elaborations on this basic design: a different coloured spine and separate corner pieces of gummed paper, for example. But if instructions are to be used as an incentive to reading, they need to be kept as simple and straightforward as possible. Individual modifications are best left to the children, although it should be pointed out that plain wrapping paper is just as suitable as wallpaper, and it can always be decorated with potato-printing or whatever appeals to the child.

A slightly more elaborate file that has the advantage of using old exercise book covers is shown in Figs. 22 & 23. The method of construction is as follows:

Get hold of two old exercise books of similar size, and remove the staples and contents. Paste brown paper over one cover, making sure that the corners are neatly turned in and mitred (A).

Now cut a slit 5″ long and $\frac{1}{10}$″ wide down the centre crease of the second cover (B); it should be equidistant from the top and bottom. Cut a strip of thickish brown paper, 10″ by 5″, and rule up as shown in C. (This strip can of course be cut from a third old cover if enough are available.)

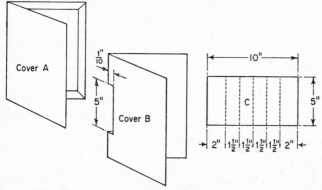

Fig. 22. The first stages in making a file.

I

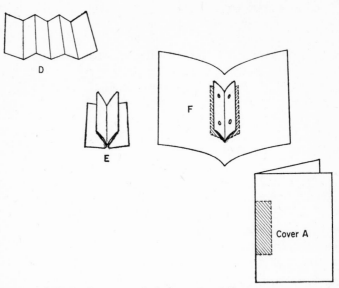

Fig. 23. The final stages and the completed file.

Fold this strip along the lines, concertina-fashion, to form the centre of the file (D). Now, leaving the two end sections free, paste the middle sections in two pairs; that is, the concertina strip will now have four sections only, the two middle ones being of double thickness (E). Punch holes through both these middle sections at top and bottom, as shown, and keeping 1″ clear of any edge. Next, from the inside of cover B, slip the two free end sections through the slit, and paste them firmly down on the outside of cover B, one on each side of the slit (F). Finally, paste cover B inside cover A and leave to dry under pressure. A shoelace or a piece of coloured string threaded through the holes completes the file.

In addition to the kind of 'personal' material that children will keep in these files, we need to encourage them to start collecting their own written work. Like the advertisements, etc., this is mounted on suitably sized sheets of paper which are punched (the children love doing this!) and then tied in place.

Amongst the most popular and useful items of early written work is the Diary. Each day children can suggest a sentence about something that has happened at home, on the way to school or in school itself. We may need to simplify their suggestions a little, but the less we interfere with what they want to write, the more effective will be the process of consolidating reading skill. How much we can learn about children through their Personal Work Books and Diaries is clear from the reproduction of the first page in a disturbed and backward child's book (Age: 9.6; Reading Age: 5.2: that is, a non-reader) facing page 96. Bill's basic need of love and affection is very clear from what he writes and draws.

Our part in the production of these books is limited to writing very lightly the words the child has suggested under the day and the date. The child goes over the script (kin-aesthetic help) and illustrates the sentence in his own way and from his own choice of illustrative materials.

These Files can also be used to form a group or class collection of 'books'. We can pin a File on the wall, and paste into it each morning the 'Word for the Day'. This word or phrase needs to be chosen for its topicality and interest— *Ice cream, A holiday tomorrow, Swimming pool, A man on the moon!*—and children soon get into the habit of looking at the file as they come into the classroom. What one child cannot read another will tell him—the Look-and-Listen Method![1]

Another file may be made in the form of an Alphabetical Folder by cutting 'steps' down the side of 26 sheets of thin card and printing a letter on the end of each step (Fig. 24). Children can then file cuttings and alliterative comic cap-

[1] See also the 'Message Method' described in Chapter 12.

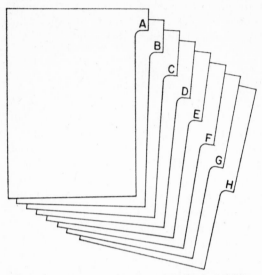

F<small>IG</small>. 24. Cards for use in an alphabetical folder.

tions (Billy Bunter, Rob Roy, Sunlight Soap) in the appropriate sections, which will give them some knowledge of the
sound values of various letters based on the rather more constant first letters of words. Some of the old spelling books
contain material that can be included, but we need to guard
against the inclusion of words that feature more than one
sound value for the same letter (a fault that detracts somewhat from the value of one of the best Alphabetical books:
Dr. Seuss's *A*, *B*, *C* where C is illustrated by '. . . Camel on
the Ceiling'). We should try to make phonics look rather
more helpful than they in fact are during these early stages,
when confidence is one of the most important factors of
success.

Files make good covers for collections. Sheets of thin card
suitably slotted can form the basis of an album, and the contents may revolve around one central theme like Transport,

or be divided up into sections such as Pets and Games. The cigarette card size picture is a little small for our purpose; the print is certainly unsuitable and, if children are keen to make a collection of this nature, we shall have to print a title or label underneath for them to trace over. Advertisements are generally the best source of file material; they use striking pictures and boldly printed, simply worded captions as a rule.

Another valuable source of more personal caption material is a box of assorted newspaper headlines. Children may look through these in groups of three or four until they find the word or words they want for a particular purpose. The teacher's help may be called for, but often there is *collectively* sufficient reading ability in the group to overcome the individual's difficulties. Sorting through headlines is good practice in word recognition; repetitive practice that is difficult to provide in other situations without the risk of boring children. If new sentences and captions are added to the collection from time to time, and again this is a way of actively involving weak readers in reading work out of school, many new words may be learnt in an incidental fashion, even though these are not the ones that the child happens to be seeking. It goes without saying that the content of headlines and phrases included may sometimes have to be quietly vetted!

Newspapers as such will not generally attract children so readily as comics, since newspapers are not geared to children's interests. But there is no reason why a file should not be made the basis of a class newspaper or newsfolder. Card subdivisions in the file can bear such headings as *Sport*, *School News*, *Personal*, *Notices*, *Advertisements*, *Riddles*, *Science* and *Things to Make*. Perhaps this is really more of a class magazine, but does this matter? The direction one of these files ultimately takes should be decided by the children and their particular interests. Their value in terms of the teaching of reading lies in the strong personal motivation to read implicit in making such material.

Other well-tried favourites are Weather Report Files, in which children compile a brief account of the day's weather, using master cards on which are printed the words that they will need (Fig. 25). This File may be operated in conjunction with a simple weather station composed of a weather vane, bottle barometer, thermometer and a crude anemometer 'to see if it's really windy out!' It is possible to adapt a funnel and jar as a rain gauge, but this tends to complicate things. The Weather File may be Purposeful Reading par excellence but our main intention, disguised though it is, remains crossing the bridge of reading to the book proper.

There are many other possible ways in which both Individual Personal Files and Collective Class Files may develop. One child will proudly show another what he has been doing, and in this way, although (or because!) these files are Personal, they will circulate in the class. More and more words will be seen, and children will become accustomed to what is at least approaching the conventional book.

The final step in this transition stage may at first sound like something of an imposition to the busy teacher—but it is to make the first printed books ourselves.

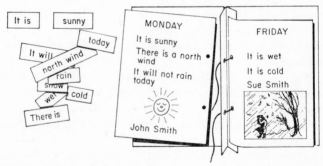

FIG. 25. A Weather Report file.

There are two ways of doing this: on a typewriter (and in this day and age, Local Authorities please note, *every* school should have a typewriter available for the use of the staff—and the one or two children who will benefit from using it as indicated in Chapter 5); secondly, with the aid of the little printing outfits that are sold to children as toys.

Writing these first books is neither as difficult nor as time-consuming as might be assumed. A typewriter is perhaps the most satisfactory method of production, since several copies can be made at the same time with carbon paper. Printing sets are better left to children to employ in reproducing their own work for perhaps the Class Magazine or their Personal Work Book.

The important points that we need to bear in mind are: (i) to keep the book short; (ii) to make it interesting; (iii) to build in a fair amount of repetition.

A child who is able to read five or six booklets of perhaps half a dozen pages each feels that he has made much more progress than if he had completed one book of 36 pages. And, anyway, it is far more difficult to write a 36-page story! The small amount of reading material in one of these books can be disguised by including an index, fly-leaves and illustrations provided by the children. In fact, a useful approach to such material is to say: 'I want you to read this little story and draw me a picture about it on each of the blank pages.' And, if the content of the story itself does prove a bit of a headache, remember that no great literary skill is required. Short, amusing or exciting incidents are being described every day in the newspapers and on TV. Simply retold, they will serve the purpose well, and may often have the added advantage of the child having heard something about them. Every school has its own 'incidents', too, and familiarity breeds attraction in these cases, besides affording a clue to many of the words used. Or we can enlist the help of children who are sufficiently ahead of the remedial group.

What basically we will be trying to do throughout this stage is to reorganise the child's emotional attitude towards the word 'book'. We need to show him the book in all its forms so that he comes to regard it in a new light. There are plenty of other types of book besides the File and Work Book. There are painting books, tracing books, autograph books, broadcast lesson books, quiz books, nature books, puzzle books, riddle books, fun books, 3-D stand-up books, comics (see Chapter 7) and all the rest of them.

Contact with this type of material should not only change the child's attitude, it should enlarge his reading vocabulary still further to the point that, knowing a number of the commonest words in children's books from V-V Multiple Reader work, and having some knowledge of crude phonic analysis from other activities we have described, plus the additional vocabulary he should have gained by this stage, he is able to stagger through the first real books he is invited to read with little or no help—but a great deal of praise—from his teacher.

Chapter 11

Reading Clubs

"There is something to be learnt from each method that has been found useful in the past."—H.M.S.O., *Primary Education*

We should now be at the point where our less able readers have made a new start with reading books manifestly different from those in which they originally failed to learn to read.

At all costs we need to preserve the atmosphere of success and the momentum of their progress forward. They should be allowed to return from time to time to reading games and apparatus, although increasingly the emphasis needs to shift from playing to making cards, games and books for those less advanced. Files and Personal Work Books should be kept going, and the contents will tend gradually to become longer and more complicated. Raising the level of difficulty, as we have seen, needs to be a very gradual process; it is far better for our children to continue to succeed with easy reading than to fail with matter that is as yet beyond their powers.

At the same time they need to be extended individually at their best rate. The sooner they are able to cope with reading sufficiently well to understand, for instance, what is on the board or what is in their school books, the sooner their level both of self-respect and general education will rise.

At first consideration this seems again a task of individual attention that is physically beyond the powers of any teacher with a whole class of children. But is the teacher always, in every situation, necessarily the only—or even the best— source of personal help? What about the children themselves?

The monitorial system devised by Lancaster and Bell in the dark ages of schooling was an attempt to solve in practical terms a problem similar in essentials to that which faces us at the moment. The answer, in the case of the Lancastrian schools, '. . . whereby about a thousand children may be taught and governed by one master only' sounds monstrous even to the teacher of today's over-large classes. But there is no doubt that Lancaster and Bell had the interests of children at heart; and, moreover, we can still learn from their fundamental premise that child can teach child.

In the freer, happier and altogether more enlightened modern classroom, with its emphasis on the child as an individual, there is still the possibility that we may neglect or underestimate the very real value of group work. Children are by nature gregarious; they walk, talk and play in groups. Although reading is an individual skill, there is still much to be gained by placing the now somewhat less-favoured 'group reading' in a new setting: the social setting of co-operation implicit in a classroom club. Why, in brief, should we not let our children help one another forward from now on through the medium of a Reading Club?

Children love societies, especially those offering facilities for the passing of tests and the gaining of badges. The psychology of such popular movements as Scouts and Guides is largely bound up with this fact. If the same principle can be applied to the teaching of backward readers, a similar measure of success may well follow.

Literally translated, this means running remedial reading

as a club in which tests and badges play a large part. The primary aim of such an organisation should be to provide an external stimulus to reading, as distinct from the basic appeal of context, yet it must be capable of unobtrusively improving mechanical word skill.

By way of a start we can give the club a colourful and appealing title with a good background potential: for example The Rangers' Reading Club. We then extend an offer of membership to the whole class and base the club's activities on the series of books at present in use. If, for example, there are 18 books in a series, institute tests for badges as follows:

Books read	Badge awarded
1	Member (no badge)
3	Cowboy
6	Ranger
9	Deputy
13	Sheriff
18	Marshal

In a Railway Reading Club, the titles might be Porter, Signalman, Foreman, Guard and Driver.

The actual tests for promotion are embodied in class reading lessons. Every child, irrespective of ability, begins with the test for membership, Book 1, and in order to pass is required to read aloud with reasonable fluency 3 pages. This means that each book in the series is read through completely five or six times, and the near non-readers, following for dear life, are afforded the maximum opportunity of picking up and remembering the sentences that will gain them their badges—and reading power into the bargain! The better readers also benefit from this process because their recognition of common words is accelerated.

Those children who fail to become Rangers are taken as a 'posse' during other reading periods by a child who has passed the test. Rangers who are unable to reach the next stage are similarly helped by a Deputy, and so on, the groups being staggered in operation so that they do not clash. Sheriffs and Marshals have the additional duty of being responsible for general law and order during these sessions. Thus class, group and individual reading is provided for within the framework of the club.

The badges are easily made. We ask the children to collect round lapel badges which various manufacturers give away as part of their advertisement schemes. Each is given a coat of white enamel so that the surface becomes blank, and then a bold C, R, D, S or M in different colours is added. More elaborate badges are of course possible, but certainly not necessary.

In addition to badges, certificates are awarded for each test passed. The child makes his own copy from a specimen provided, and will obviously take great pains with his handwriting. It pays, therefore, to let him make as many copies as he wishes, trying to improve on each one. If the phrasing of different certificates is varied slightly, a few extra words are absorbed by the child as he progresses. A typical certificate might read:

This is to show that.........................
is a member of the Rangers' Reading Club, and having
read........books, is hereby made a..............
(Signed)...................(President)

Sheriffs and Deputies may be given warrants on the same lines, while Marshals can 'run for Presidency'.

Another device that assists vocabulary is the employment of passwords. At the end of the afternoon the password for the following day is presented to members in sentence form via the blackboard:

The password for Wednesday is BOOK.

The whole sentence is duly copied down by members in

their writing books and the password itself written on a slip
of paper which is carried around and used during the next
day. Simple English exercises involving the word may be
set, and of course no harm is done if the children learn to
spell it! Five passwords are given per week, and by the end
of the term a further helpful list of common words has been
compiled. Being able to read the current password is something that every child will wish to do, and felt need is a
wonderful incentive.

Proficiency tests in the form of word lists connected with
some aspect of the club can be introduced, and these may
be put together on a phonic basis with advantage. A proficiency test in Horsemanship would consist of knowing and
being able to use in sentences 5 or 10, say, S and T words,
if work with these particular sounds was wanted:

> S: saddle, spurs, stable, stall, stirrup
> T: tame, tough, teach, timid, tumble

Such tests should carry no award apart from kudos. Over-
complication can result in a reading club where there is no
time to read! The tests do, however, make word list and
sound work more interesting, and therefore more effective.

We can go further and draw up a set of rules dealing with
duties, privileges, proficiency and badge tests, and out-of-
school activities, if these are contemplated. From the large
copy which will be hung up in the classroom, the children
will be able to write their own membership cards. What these
will contain apart from personal memoranda and rules is
arbitrary; it is worth bearing in mind that they will be, in
effect, miniature personal reading books, and that the contents will be read repeatedly.

Whenever a lesson has a connection, however remote, with
the club, a special Club News Sheet is produced. This is
merely notes on the lesson reduced to simply worded sentences, perhaps with a touch of 'club flavouring' added. It is

copied from the blackboard by the children, and used as supplementary (and informatory) reading material.

The club in itself provides scope for many other lessons. A background of History, Geography and sometimes elementary Science will be needed so that the children can relate their club to reality. For those of us who favour projects, it will throw up natural yet original lines of enquiry.

One final point: a club of this nature can be *fun* as well as functional.

Chapter 12

Simplicity Spells Success

"Teaching reading through current experiences retold in a child's own language . . . is the only safeguard for slow learners to prevent reading lessons from degenerating into monotonous, formal drill exercises."—Hildreth: *Learning the Three R's*

Whilst the schemes, approaches and techniques we have discussed so far should at least have opened up new lines of thought in practical reading, and whilst it is to be hoped that amongst the ideas put forward most of us will have found something that is worth trying, we should bear in mind that any given approach will depend for its success on the enthusiasm of the teacher behind it.

If we believe in a certain practical approach, then ten to one it will work—for us. If we have little faith in a method, then ten to one it will prove to be unsatisfactory—for us. The same principle applies to the use of reading schemes.

Now it may well be that some of us would prefer much simpler suggestions. As a profession we are a traditionally cautious and conventional set of people, unwilling to throw overboard methods and beliefs that we have subscribed to for any length of time. And, of course, any experienced teacher recognises that the less complicated a method or approach the more likely it is to succeed.

For those who believe that simplicity spells success, let us put forward for consideration three suggestions which are basic, down-to-earth ways of helping non-readers forward, using little, and indeed in one case no, apparatus, and founded on conventional, well established teaching methods.

Let us begin with 'Reading by Messages', which is really an extension of the use of the humble flash card. Flash card work, the recognition of individual words written in large print on cards, and held up at random by the teacher, can be of great use in helping the less able reader forward, provided that the material used is interesting and the technique of using flash cards is disguised so that it is not associated with the work of this nature going on in the Infant School.

The speed element of recognition is something that we are not unduly worried about when using flash cards with less able readers. We are naturally far more concerned with the primary skill of word recognition; with the absorption of the word shape so that its 'face' will become familiar enough to be recognised again. Speed is a later consideration.

'Reading by Messages' turns on the use of a message as the basis of a flash card exposed for some time. We shall need a holder for our message, and this is quickly constructed from a large manila envelope, in the front of which a slit is cut

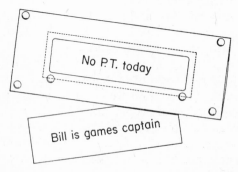

FIG. 26. 'Reading by Messages.'

approximately 10″ by 3″ (Fig. 26). We shall in fact need three or four of these holders, and they should be pinned up in the classroom at points where children cannot fail to notice them as they move about in the course of entry, exit, changing classrooms, going to cupboards, etc. The ideal location is at eye level on doors.

Immediately above the slit we can print boldly: TODAY'S MESSAGE. About half an inch below the slit, we shall need to stick two extra drawing pins through the envelope so that the eleven-by-four-inch card strips bearing the actual messages will have something to support them as they slide into position through the end of the envelope. The flap can be cut off or tucked in behind the strip.

First thing each morning we duplicate the message for the day on three of these card strips and slip them into position. The messages should be as brief as possible, and may follow some common theme that can be changed from month to month if desired. Suppose that Sport is selected. Then a typical selection of messages for one week might run:

> Brenda is Netball Captain.
> Tom scored two goals yesterday.
> Yesterday Wolves lost two—one.
> No P.T. today.
> Football practice at four o'clock.

Hobbies, Riddles, School Gossip, Current Affairs, Weather Reports and Space News are other popular topics. Another possibility, particularly at a later stage, is to turn the daily message into a sort of serial story, one sentence per day. The first books prepared by the teacher (see Chapter 9) can be used as a basis for this work with very obvious advantages. However, let us consider how the basic idea of a daily message works as far as a non-reader is concerned.

Children coming into the classroom will find it difficult to avoid reading the message out loud; in fact we must tacitly

K

encourage this, even if there is a bit of a buzz as a result! The non-reader, only too anxious to conform in this respect, hears what the message says and dutifully repeats it, or 'reads' it for the benefit of his neighbour. Provided that the duplicate messages have been strategically placed, he is able to do this repeatedly during the school day, and thus he stands a very good chance of becoming familiar enough with the words in the sentence to recognise them at a later date: really to be able to read them.

At the end of the afternoon, the backward readers copy the message for the day into a book kept specially for this purpose, or in a file (see Chapter 9 again). In the course of a few weeks this collection of messages, complete with suitable pictures drawn by the children, has turned into a personal reading book, or work book, full of material that not only relates to things that actually concern the readers, but which they have had the opportunity of reading by Look-and-Say.

This collection may form the basis of the essential sight vocabulary that the backward readers need to acquire in order to provide both a starting point for reading and a higher degree of self-confidence, or it may be used as supplementary material. And a point that should recommend the approach to the busy class teacher—it is largely self-operative!

The next of these simpler suggestions is concerned with Visual Aids for backward readers. The Message is in some respects a visual aid, but this second approach is essentially visual, in that it consists of the construction of various 'pictures' hung round the classroom and composed entirely of words.

The Word Charts which form the basis of these 'pictures' are best constructed by the children themselves. They may collect words from newspapers, magazines and comics, cutting them out and sticking them in the appropriate spaces indicated on a master copy made by the teacher. They may trace or copy words and this will mean rough copies and repeated attempts to reach a good enough standard for exhibition to the rest of the class. In this way repetitive practice and kinaesthetic reinforcement may be obtained without boredom. Again, this is an activity that less able children can get on with by themselves during the time that their teacher is occupied with other groups.

Useful charts include:

    25 common words (Fig. 27)
    25 three-letter words
    10 common phrases (Fig. 27)

25 COMMON WORDS				
I	a	the	and	an
he	she	it	you	we
my	to	is	in	of
look	here	this	have	play
dog	boy	girl	that	Christmas

10 COMMON PHRASES
Goal!   Offside!   Shoot!   Penalty!
That was the week that was
Danger! Keep Out! Private! No Entry!
Beware of the dog

FIG. 27.

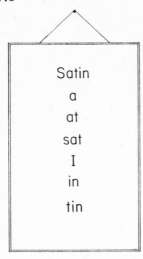

Fig. 28.

10 local place names (from looking at the words on the way to school—streets, parks, houses, etc.)

25 traffic signs and directions, collected in the same way

10 advertisement slogans (for example, Sharp's the toffee—Sharp's the word!)

Long words broken down into smaller words that are contained in them (Fig. 28)

Personal sound charts, which are simply phonic picture alphabets built up by the children around words that interest them, as distinct from the type of *A for Ant* and *B for Bunny* (although these examples may be suitable for a child interested in animals or nature)

An example of a personal sound chart is shown facing page 97. It was the work of a Word-blind boy of 11 (reading age then 6·4) who had a passion for aeroplanes. He could copy pictures beautifully, though unable to draw without their aid. In copying each picture, he was absorbing the initial sound of the letter concerned.

The way to success is through words chosen by the children, rather than those *we* think should interest them.

When the charts are finished, children can turn their attention to making 'real pictures' of them. This process begins with unearthing the stack of old framed photographs showing the netball team of 1906, etc., that lies neglected and unwanted in a drawer or corner in most schools. If this is not available, an appeal may be made to the children to have a look at home for anything similar that may be unwanted and their parents will allow them to bring along to enjoy a new lease of life in the classroom.

The backing paper will have to be taken off, and the old rusty tacks holding the picture in place removed with pliers. The pictures themselves can of course be put back in their original resting place if there is any question of wanting to preserve them further, but the glass will probably have to come out and be thoroughly washed and polished with a soft cloth. The wooden frame will be improved by a little attention of this sort, and a touch of school floor polish.

If at this stage none of the completed charts will fit the

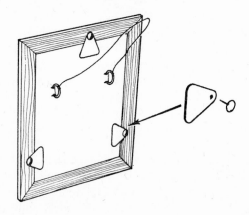

FIG. 29. 'Quick release' fittings.

frames, so much the better. The children can cut sheets of white card to the correct size and produce improved or modified replicas of the original 'pictures'. Finally they can put the chart in the frame, replace the card backing and make 'quick release' fittings (Fig. 29) held in place with drawing pins, so that if someone wants to improve or modify a chart even further, it can be changed over with little or no difficulty.

Again, all this will decrease the drain on the teacher's time and increase the less able children's progress in proportion, because they will always have worth-while and interesting practical activities to hand. The words and the sounds have every chance of being driven home through the concentration that pleasurable work with a tangible end-product will produce. They can also be used as starting points for written work, especially first attempts at creative writing.

When a chart is taken out of a picture for replacement, it may still be used as a Visual Aid in the form of a Wall-Book. The Wall-Book is a chart cut vertically through the centre, the two sides being hinged by a strip of rag glued to the back. One side is then pinned to the wall and the other folds over it to close the 'book', the end being slipped under the edge of a drawing pin.

Although the Wall-Book has the disadvantage of being shut when not in use, it does attract a surprising number of children through the very business of opening and shutting it. Sound charts are particularly suited to this piece of apparatus, since children can then make a routine of going to a particular Wall-Book in groups for a short period during each reading-lesson.

The last of our three suggestions is the simplest of all. It needs no apparatus beyond pencil and paper, and it is in many ways a 'last ditch' method when everything else has failed. It is an individual approach, and demands a certain amount of the teacher's time for a short, regular period of help every day. We may call it the 'Translation' method.

With this, we ask the child to try to write a line or two on anything that is of interest to him. The result, if he is a near non-reader, will probably be either nonsense syllables or hieroglyphics, but this does not matter; all we want him to do is to put *something* on paper.

Then we ask the child to 'read' his piece aloud. Whether he accomplishes this by memory or imagination is immaterial; all we want him to do is to tell us what he would have put down correctly had he been able to do so. We praise his efforts, look at the 'writing' and blandly suggest that although he is able to 'read' his work it might be easier for everyone, including him, if the actual writing was a little neater. We then offer to write the piece out again so that he can see what we mean.

This we do, 'translating' the child's original (!) work with his aid, which undoubtedly will prove very necessary, into bold script. Then we invite him to try 'reading' this revised version, and the process then becomes a variation of look-and-say again.

The next step is to supply the child with tracing paper and get him to trace the correct words on to a clean sheet of paper, which will, of course, help him further with the process of assimilating the word patterns. He will probably need to go over the finished tracing again with a pencil, which will provide still more help, and then he draws a suitable picture to add to the enjoyment, and to create a picture clue as to what these words say should he forget. The sheet goes into a Personal Word Book or File.

Gradually, day by day, the translations will grow into a miniature book. The limited vocabulary of the child will impose a certain amount of repetition which is highly desirable, and his teacher, by a little tactful guidance of expression, can further this. Brevity is of paramount importance in the early stages.

When reading confidence has been established, and recognition of a small basic vocabulary attained, work sheets can be introduced to be used in conjunction with the pieces that the child is now able to read. These will take the form of a few questions that are as repetitive as possible without becoming boring, plus, perhaps, some simple activity instructions; for example:

WORK SHEET on MY TOY GARAGE

Answer words: Yes   No

1. Have you a garage?   (Answers at first will consist of
2. Is it a toy garage?   a plain *Yes* or *No* and these
3. Is it big?   words must be provided as
4. Is it little?   models. Later, an expanded
5. Is it painted?   answer using the same words—
                       Yes, I have a garage—should
                       be produced.)

Things to do

1. Draw your garage.
2. Draw some cars.
3. Paint your garage.
4. Paint some cars.
   Paint the garage red.
   Paint the cars black.
   Paint the pumps red.

The 'translation method', judged by the standards of our other suggestions, is simple to the point of crudity. Simplicity is, we should remember, the keynote of these three final approaches, and indeed there is nothing to indicate that complexity is at all necessary to success in practical reading.

The real necessity in any technique remains the enthusiastic and above all understanding teacher behind it.

Chapter 13

Mainly for Students

"I care not whether I teach or whether I am taught so long as the truth prevails."—Comenius

---

Amongst those who have followed us through this book are, we may hope, parents and teachers-to-be who are looking into the pitfalls and possibilities of practical reading.

This is a very good thing on a number of counts. Student teachers should realise as early on in their careers as possible that the teaching of reading is a complex process which demands a great deal of knowledge, patience and skill. They should follow up their academic discovery of this fact with visits to and observation of Infant classes, and discussions with experienced Infant teachers, whose knowledge of practical reading will put theory into its correct perspective.

Ideally, since reading is fundamentally necessary at all stages of education, students (and all teachers for that matter) should have some first-hand experience of teaching young children to read before they begin to think in terms of trying to re-teach those who have failed.

There is a tendency in some schools to place the teacher straight from College with a class of Slow Learners; the Progress Class, or the D stream, or whatever they may be called. This is patently unfair both to the new teacher and to the children he is called upon to deal with. 'He (or she)

can't do much damage there' is not only a callous, cynical and unenlightened attitude, it is often a tragically mistaken one, because without either knowledge or experience the new teacher may do irreparable damage to the children's educational potential and to his own educational outlook.

With sufficient teaching practice and a handful of techniques, the newly qualified teacher will at least be aware of the difficulties facing him; and, we may hope, perhaps in a stronger position to do something constructive about the situation, and our informed parents can back him up.

Since students may seek some form of summary that will satisfy examiners—and this we must whisper—who may or may not have had much practical experience in the proving ground of the classroom, may we be forgiven for including a happy little diagram to this end.

'The Tractor of Reading Backwardness', besides having a pleasant alliterative ring, does suggest something slow-moving yet powerful, which is akin to remedial techniques. There are, as we have stressed, no slick, easy short cuts to success.

Beginning at the front of the tractor, we have a starting handle, interest. Without interest, a child cannot get started. Once we have interest going (and the starting handle can be very, very stiff) the engine (intelligence) comes to life, but if the oil (success) is thick or lacking, then the engine will be unable to produce anything like full power. It may even seem to seize up, so we should pay a great deal of attention to the lubrication of intelligence by success.

Another component that affects the engine's potential is the fan-belt (physical condition). A slack fan-belt can cause overheating and if the child gets 'het up' in this way it will again inhibit his intellectual potential. The fan-belt is also responsible for charging the battery via the dynamo, and so poor physical condition has a link with the lamps (visual skills). The exhaust note (aural skills) reminds us of the part

THE TRACTOR OF READING BACKWARDNESS

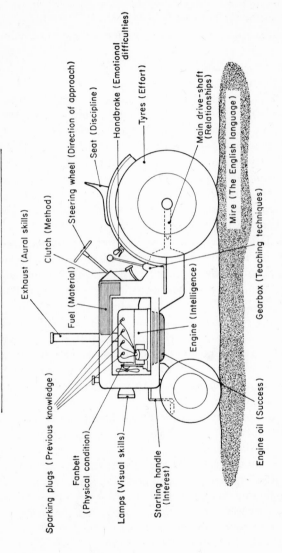

Exhaust (Aural skills)

Clutch (Method)

Steering wheel (Direction of approach)

Seat (Discipline)

Handbrake (Emotional difficulties)

Tyres (Effort)

Main drive-shaft (Relationships)

Mire (The English language)

Fuel (Material)

Engine (Intelligence)

Gearbox (Teaching techniques)

Sparking plugs (Previous knowledge)

Fanbelt (Physical condition)

Lamps (Visual skills)

Starting handle (Interest)

Engine oil (Success)

the ear has to play in learning to read. We must be on the look out for an uneven exhaust, although this is sometimes caused by dirty plugs (previous experience with spoken language or the lack of it). The sounds of words may be meaningless if not sparked into life by a practical knowledge of what they stand for.

The first task of the engine is to turn fuel (the material read) into power (understanding). Power is difficult to draw and so we have left it to the imagination or to the originality of the doodling pencil. The effectiveness of the power depends on a number of related components: the gear box (techniques) and the clutch (method). An unsuitable method is very much like a slipping clutch, and in effect rather like having the handbrake (emotional difficulties) on. The tractor cannot go forward like this very easily, and a great deal of friction and heat develops, causing diminished efficiency.

How much of the power is available at the wheels depends on the main drive-shaft (relationships). A child who knows that the teacher is interested in him as a person and who in turn likes and respects his teacher, is so much more likely to go forward irrespective of the general direction of the approach as shown on our diagram by the steering wheel. But the teacher cannot do all the work. The tractor must have good solid tyres (effort) in order to progress through the slippery, unhelpful mire of the English language, undrained as yet by i.t.a.

And one small but necessary final point. In order to be in full control, it is necessary that the teacher is firmly in the seat (discipline).

So much, then, for our theoretical summary, the Tractor of Reading Backwardness. But in terms of practical reading we cannot do better than to repeat once more the final fact in the section dealing with a suggested approach:

"It is primarily you, not your techniques or my techniques, that will lay the foundations of success in reading."

Some Thoughts to End With

One of the most difficult things to do as regards Education is to forecast future developments. Finance, politics, expediency and prejudice bend if not warp what is to happen in the schools of tomorrow with a fine disregard for the practical requirements of children.

However, let us end by attempting to look forward to the end of the century. What will the common denominator of the teaching or reading be by then?

Judging by the tremendous amount of concern over literacy currently, and the various long-term experiments in progress, we may hope with a fair degree of confidence that ground will have been gained. One of the greatest future contributions to progress in reading and at the same time one of the simplest, would be to reduce the size of Primary School classes. Yet, glancing at the legislation ahead, it is hard to see how this will be brought about by present plans and policies.

As to method, have we in fact anything to add to the concluding comment that Dr. J. Roswell Galagher made in a broadcast interview relating to specific difficulties in reading:

"Prevention is *always* better than cure"?

Perhaps i.t.a. has the answer. As a boy who is succeeding with reading for the first time at the age of ten scribbled in the back of the i.t.a. books responsible for his success:

> twist and shout, twist and shout
> ie noe whot this books about;
> hip, hip, hip, hip, hip hoorae
> three big cheerz for i.t.a.
>   Amen?

Bibliography

A few useful books:

Success and Failure in Learning to Read, R. Morris (Oldbourne, 1963)

Reading in the Primary School, J. Morris (Newnes, 1963)

Reading Disability, Hermann (Ryerson Press, Canada, 1959)

Backwardness in Reading, M. D. Vernon (Cambridge, 1958)

Teaching Children to Read, J. C. & M. F. Gagg (Newnes, 1955)

The Psychology and Teaching of Reading, 4th edn., F. J. Schonell (Oliver & Boyd, 1961)

The Teaching of Reading and Writing, W. S. Gray (Unesco, 1956)

Teaching Backward Pupils, S. S. Segal (Evans, 1963)

Some useful tests:

The Standard Reading Tests, J. C. Daniels & H. Diack (Chatto & Windus)

The Holborn Reading Scale, A. F. Watts (Harrap)

Graded Word Reading Test, F. J. Schonell (Oliver & Boyd)

Graded Word Reading Test, P. E. Vernon (U.L.P.)

The Burt (Rearranged) Word Reading Test, P. E. Vernon (U.L.P.)

The Sentence Reading Test, Watts (N.F.E.R.-Newnes)